Vedic Theory
of
The Origin of Speech

By

Dr. Ravi Prakash Arya

Joseph Skulj

Indian Foundation for Vedic Science
1051, Sector-1, Rohtak, Haryana, India Ph: 01262-292580
(Rohtak) Delhi Contact No. 09313033917; 09650183260
Email:vedicscience@rediffmail.com
vedicscience@hotmail.com;
Website : www.vedascience.com

Second Edition

Kali era: 5115 (c. 2014)
Kalpa era : 1,97,29,49,115
Brahma era: 15,55,21,97,29,49,115

ISBN 81- 87710-61-6

Contents

	Page
Preface	5
Introduction	9
Types of Speech	12
Origin of *Ākhyātas* or Action Sounds	15
Origin of Names (Agent Sounds)	39
Divine Origin of Speech	43
Origin of Vedas	48
Sequence of Evolution of Phonemes	54
Origin and Evolution of European Languages	73
Phonological Analysis	73
Morphological Analysis	79
Evolution of the Lithuanian Language	131
Evolution of the Avesta Language	133
Evolution of the Greek Language	138
Evolution of the Latn Language	140
Evolution of Old Slav. and other Slavic languages	142
Vedic Origin of Numbers in the World Languages	148
Initial Mutations in Vedic Family of Lnguages	174
Review of the idea of Classification of IE Languages as Centum and Satam group	178
Vedic Family of Languages	183
References	185

Preface

Linguistics, the scientific study of language, can reach more deeply into the human past than the most ancient written records. It compares related languages to reconstruct their immediate progenitors and eventually their ultimate ancestor, or proto-language. The proto-language in turn illuminates the lives of its speakers and locates them in time and place.

The science developed from the study of the Vedic (Indo-European) family of languages, by far the largest in number of languages and number of speakers. Nearly half of the world's population speaks Vedic (Indo-European) family of language as a first language; six of the 10 languages in which Scientific American appears-English, French, German, Italian, Russian and Spanish-belong to this family.

Our work indicates that the Vedic (Sanskrit) originated in India and other language of European or Indian family originated as daughter languages when the Sanskrit speaking Indians migrated to various parts of western hemisphere from time to time. This subject will be discussed exclusively in our forthcoming book 'Origin of Indo Europeans'.

The reconstruction of ancient languages may be likened to the method used by molecular biologists in their quest to understand the evolution of life. The biochemist identifies molecular elements that perform similar functions in widely divergent species to infer the characteristics of the primordial cell from which they are presumed to have descended. So does the linguist seek correspondences in grammar, syntax, vocabulary and vocalization among known languages in order to reconstruct their immediate forebears and ultimately the original tongue. Living languages can be compared directly with one another; dead languages that have survived in written form can usually be vocalized by inference from internal linguistic evidence. Phonology-the study of word sounds-is all-important to historical linguists because sounds are more stable over the centuries than are meanings.

Early studies of Vedic (Indo-European) family of

languages focused on those languages that were most familiar to the original European researchers: the Italic, Celtic, Germanic, Baltic and Slavic families. Affinities between these and the "Indian" languages spoken in far away India were noticed by European travellers as early as the 16th century. That they might all share a common ancestor was first proposed in 1786 by Sir William Jones, an English jurist and student of eastern cultures. He thus launched what came to be known as the Indo-European hypothesis, which served as the principal stimulus to the founders of historical linguistics in the 19th century. In fact, now the time has come that the name indo European can be re-christened as Vedic family of languages.

Armenia's State Museum, in Yerevan's Republic Square, houses thousands of artefacts of early Vedic culture found throughout the territory of Armenia. The collection, biggest in the world in its number and variety has many artefacts dating back to as far as so-called Stone Age. One of the treasures of the museum is carts, or pulling wagons, dating back to early second millennium BC. The wagons along with hundreds of other artefacts such as spears, swords, arrowheads and pottery, were found from the archaeological dig at Lchashen, near Lake Sevan. The wagons for the most part have been preserved carefully and are relatively in good condition. They are the oldest surviving carts of such sort in the European world.

More recent evidence now places the probable origin of the Indo-European language from Sanskrit of India via western Asia. Three generations of archaeologists and linguists have thus far excavated and deciphered manuscripts close to a dozen ancient languages from sites in modern Turkey and as far east as Tocharia, in modern Turkistan. Their observations, together with new ideas in pure linguistic theory, have made it necessary to revise the canons of linguistic evolution.

The route of migrations of Sanskrit speaking Indian lie somewhere in the crescent that curves around the southern shores of the Black Sea, south from the Balkan peninsula, east across ancient Anatolia (today the non-European territories of Turkey) and north to the Caucasus Mountains. Here the agricultural revolution created the food surplus that impelled the migrants from

India to found villages and city-states from which, about 6,000 years ago, they began their migrations over the Eurasian continent and into history. Here it may not out of context to quote from a paper by Casey C. Bennet and Frederika A. Kaestle titled '*Reanalysis of Eurasian Population History: Ancient DNA Evidence of Population Affinities*', which was published in Human Biology, August 2006 v. 78 no. 4, pp. 413-440. There it states:

"Adding to this debate are the various theories of Indo-European origins and expansions, as argued by Mallory and Renfrew as well as numerous others. The main component of these theories is that the Indo-Europeans originally represented a centralized cultured group, although the location of their origins and the time of their dispersal and expansion as well as possible routes are greatly debated. Whereas Renfrew has argued for an Anatolian origin connected to the spread of Neolithic farming, an alternative argument is detailed by Mallory, Gimbutas and others, who connect the Indo-Europeans to the southern Russian steppe, possibly around the Black Sea and/or the Caspian Sea as well as the southern Urals or northern Caucasus and/or possibly Eastern Europe...."

In our forthcoming paper we (Joseph Skulj and co-authors), are making a case, based on linguistic, genetic and zoo archaeological evidence that the Indo-Aryans and Slavs have their origin in the Indus Valley, not Europe, and that their split occurred before the origin of farming. The genetic spread, however, took place north of the Black Sea. This is not to say that the cultural influence was not present south of the Black Sea.

It appears that some of the migrants reached Anatolia from the India around 2000 B.C. and established the Hittite kingdom, which held all of Anatolia in its power by 1400 B.C. Its official language was among the first of the Indo-European languages to find its way into writing. Early in this century, Bedrich Hrozny, a linguist at Vienna University and later at Charles University in Prague, deciphered Hittite inscriptions (written in cuneiform, the ancient writing system based on wedge-shaped symbols) on tablets that had been found in the library of the capital at Hattusas, 200 kilometres east of modern Ankara. The library also contained cuneiform tablets in two related languages: Luwian and Palaic. The evolution of Luwian could be traced in later hieroglyphic inscriptions made around 1200 B.C., after the fall of the Hittite

Empire. To this emerging family of Anatolian languages linguists added Lydian (closer to Hittite) and Lycian (closer to Luwian), known from inscriptions dating back to late in the first millennium B.C.

The appearance of Hittite and other Anatolian languages at the turn of the third to the second millennium B.C. sets an absolute chronological limit for the break-up of the Vedic language. It can be maintained that Anatolian departed from the parent Sanskrit no later than the fourth millennium B.C. and possibly much earlier.

Dr. Ravi Prakash Arya

Joseph Skulj

Introduction

When we take up the study of language, the first and foremost question arises as to how when and where the language originated. More the linguists troubled their head in this direction, less they achieved success. So far it has remained an unsolved conundrum. The more it was solved, the more it became complex. Now many linguistic societies in the world have banned to raise this question again on the forum. Vedic (Indo-European) family of languages being the ancient most of all the families of languages of the world. If we are able to search the root of Indo-European Languages, the problem of the origin and evolution of almost all the languages of the world will be solved. Among the hosts of theories put forwarded on the origin of speech, one is regarding the divine origin of speech. So long it has been contended by almost all the scholars both at home and abroad that the Vedas are the propounder of this theory. In this connection a number of observations made by Vedic seers have been cited, e.g.

> 'Sanskrit is the scientifically standardized language grammatically defined by great Ṛṣis.'[1]
>
> 'Scholars created a standardized language, it was spoken earlier by various illiterate persons.'[2]
>
> 'As a result of the operation/yajñja, the standardisation of language, *Ṛgveda*, *Sāmaveda*, *Yajurveda* and *Atharvaveda* were documented.'[3]
>
> 'The statement by an expert most person in a particular field can be taken as evidence.'[4]
>
> 'Owing to the three forms of matter: *Agni* (energy in the observer space), *Vāyu* (field particles in the intermediate

---

[1] *'saṁskritaṁ nāma daivī vāganvākhyātā maharṣibhiḥ'*

[2] *'daivīṁ vācamayajanta devāḥ tāṁ viśvarupāḥ paśvo vadanti*
(*RV.* 8.100.11

[3] *'tasmāt yajñāt sarvahuta ṛcaḥ sāmāni jajñire*
chandāṁsi tasmād yajus-tasmād ajāyata' (*VS.* 31.7)

[4] *'āptopadeśaḥ śabdaḥ'* (*Nyāya Śāstra* :1.1)

space) and Ravi (light in the light space), three Vedas- *Ṛgveda*, *Yajurveda* and *Sāmaveda* - evolved for the accomplishment of *yajña* (the process of creation).'[1]

'On account of three forms of energy (*tapta*) in three spaces, three Vedas or couplets of knowledge came into being. On account of *Agni* (energy in observer space) came into being couplets called *Ṛcas* or *Ṛgveda*, on account of *Vāyu* (field or electric force in intermediate space) came into being *Yajuṣas* or *Yajuveda* and on account of *Sūrya* (light in light space) came into being *Sāmaveda* or *Sāmans.*'[2]

'The couplets that are known as *Ṛgveda*, *Yajuveda*, *Sāmaveda* and *Atharvaveda* are the exhalations of the created world.'[3]

Simply quoting these observations without understanding the actual intended sense of the speakers, everybody assumed without applying mind that they support the divine origin of speech. Nobody least bothered about the real meaning of divine and about the system or method that was followed to determine the origin of various names/words' etc. by the ancient Indian etymologists and other authorities who discussed at length the factors behind the origin of various names.

The present paper, as it does, instead of treading the bitten track and going by the repeated statements on the divine origin of speech, prefers to make and humble reappraisal of the observations of Vedic seers in the light of etymological method of inquiry adopted by ancient Indian etymologists, linguists and grammarians in determining the primitive origin of language. It also re-interprets and establishes the relevancy of the citations quoted above and others as well with regard to the Vedic theory of the origin of

---

1 *'agni vāyuravibhyastu trayaṁ brama sanātanam*
dudoha yajña siddhyarthamṛgyajuḥ sāma lakṣaṇam'
(*Śvetāśvatara Upaniṣad,* 6.18)

2 *'tebhyastaptevhyastrayo vedājayānta agnerṛgvedo*
vāyoryajurvedaḥ sūryāt sāmavedaḥ' (*Śatapatha Brāhmaṇa,* 11.5.4.10)

3 *'evaṁ vā are' sya mahatobhūtasya niḥśvasitam*
etadyadṛgvedo yajurvedaḥ sāmavedo' tharvāṅgirasaḥ' (*Ś.Br.* 11.5.8.3)

speech deduced on the basis of etymological method of inquiry and thus tries to present the actual picture behind the caption 'Divine Origin of Speech'

Types of Speech

Vedic visionaries divided the whole linguistic phenomenon into two types, viz *parā* and *aparā*.

Parā-vāk

Parā-vāk or para-speech was studied purely as a psychological phenomenon. Though it was an unarticulated speech (*avyakta-vāk*), it was also used to convey the speakers' intention, it was transmitted at the mental level or *Manomayakoṣa.* A person sitting at one place was able to transmit his message to another person setting at another place through the mental waves or the waves of consciousness activated by the power of *saṁkalpa* (will). In fact, the consciousness is also pervading the whole universe like that of matter in the form of electrons. However, this type of communication is not possible by a laity. Only the Yogis or Ṛṣ is who completely master their mental faculties through concentration and contemplation are able to communicate through *parā-vāk* or para-speech.

In the modern times, the communication has though been made fast through wireless, telephone and satellite controls, it has become expensive and one had to depend upon so many apparatuses and other operators. Also the use of mobiles phones is causing health hazards due to the radiation emitted by them. On the other hand, communication through telepathy needn't the expense of a single mite and anybody's help. It requires no media like telephones, satellite, etc. Communication through telepathy is possible from one country to another country, from one planet to another planet. It has no radiation effect.

Aparā-vāk :

Aparā-Vāk or *vyakta-vāk* (articulate speech) was studied as a physiological phenomenon, since the Vedic seers meant by *aparā-vāk* the *vyakta-vāk* or articulate speech. Before a speech is articulated at physiological level, it passes through two stages. First one being the *paśyanti* (visual) stage. At this stage, an individual with inquisitive perception visualises some physical action in the objects/things around him in his own idiosyncratic way.

At the second stage, i.e. at the stage of *madhyamā-vāk*, the physical actions are imprinted in his mind in the form of concept (*pratyaya*).

The Vedic seer (*Aitareya Brāhmaṇa*, 12.13) had it as :

> 'He appreciates the visualised object. Thus by appreciating some object or thing, one registers the *saṁskāra* (imprint) of the action of visualised object in his mind in the form of some concept'.[1]

In fact, *pratyaya* or concept may be called as a psychological action. Bhartṛhari (*Vākyapadīya*, 1.116), a great ancient linguist of India defines the concept or *pratyaya* as an internal, or psychological awareness that gets registered in the consciousness.[2] It is often articulated in the form of sounds.

Further he observes:

> 'There is no such concept in the world as can be expressed/articulated without sound. All concepts or conceptualized actions get their release only by way of sounds (uttered by men or animals)'.[3]

This process of conversion of actions into sounds (action sounds) may be illustrated as under:

Perception of action present in the object outside

↓

Conceptualization of the subject action, or concept formation in mind.

---

[1] *taṁ madhyamayā vācā śaṁsati. ātmānameva tat saṁskurute.*

[2] *'athedamāntaraṁ jñānaṁ sukṣmavāgātmanā sthitaṁ*
vyaktaye svasya rūpasya sabdatvena vivaratate.

[3] *'na so'sti pratyayo loke yaḥ śabdānugamād*
anuviddhamiva jñanaṁsarvaṁ śabdena bhāsate

(This may also be known as conversion of physical action into psychological action)

↓

Articulation/expression of concept into sounds/action sounds by perceiver.

'(This process may be known as the conversion of psychological action into physiological action.)

The action sounds or sounds thus articulated or expressed in the very beginning were called by ancient linguists or etymologists as *ākhyātās* (literally meaning expressed or articulated sounds). Since the *ākhyātas* or action sounds embodied in them the concept of the action present in the outside object at the time of its perception, it was invariably described by ancient Indian linguists or etymologists (*Nirukta,* 3.4) as *bhāva* (action) dominated.[1]

Mādhva, the author of *Dhātuvṛtti* (Bhvādigaṇa. P.21) also takes *bhāva* as concept behind coining of a root. According to him, concept consists of the meaning of the root.[2]

In fact, those *ākhyātas* were the first type of the articulate speech.

---

[1] *bhāvapradhānam ākhyātam.*

[2] *bhāvastu kevalo dhātvarthaḥ*

Origin of Ākhyātas
or
Action Sounds

At this stage one may like to know as to how the *ākhyātas* or action sounds originated.

As per observations of the Vedic seers, the *ākhyātas* or action sounds originated first in the form or monosyllabic or disyllabic onomatopoetic utterances.

> 'The speech was first articulated in monosyllables or disyllables.'[1]

The *Ātharvaṇa* seer (7.4.3.1.) also points out to this onomatopoetic character of the *ākhyātas* or action sounds. He had it as:

> 'The three forms of speech, i.e. *parā*, *paśyanti* and *madhyamā* are located in *antaḥkaraṇa* (mind), but the fourth one appeared in the form of onomatopoetic utterances.'[2]

Thus it is clear form the observations of Vedic seer that the very first *ākhyatas* (action sounds) originated in the form of onomatopoetic utterances.

One more question attached to this question is, what were the reasons or causes that led the human beings or animals articulate sounds in the beginning? Whether it was some divine intuition that made the primitive beings utter sounds or something else. It was not divine intuition that made the primitive beings pronounce sounds. It was rather the imitation of natural sounds outside that inspired the primitive men and animals utter sounds.

One of the Vedic seers (*Ṛgveda*, 7.103.1) replies this as:

---

[1] *etaṁ vācaṁ prajāpatiḥ prathamaṁ vācaṁ vyāharad ekākṣaraṁ dvayākṣaram.*

[2] *śvās ta ekā aśvās ta ekāḥ sarvā bibharti sumanasyamānāḥ tisro vāco nihitā antarsmin tāsām ekāvipapātā nughoṣam.*

'The frogs pronounce sounds inspired by the clouds.'[1]

Similarly, first man started his language with some onomatopoetic sounds. Pāṇini has also taken a good note of this type of human tendency in the following *sūtras.*

anukaraṇaṁ cānitiparam (1.4.62)

avyaktānukarṇād dvayajavarārdhādanitau ḍā ca (5.4.57)

lohitādibhyaḥ kyaṣa (3.1.13)

avyaktānukaraṇasyāt itau (6.1.98)

Pāṇini himself has discovered a long list of such sounds as were produced in the nature. Since these sounds were not expressed or articulated by any living being with some intention and since they originated in vague form in nature, they were called *avyakta* or vague sounds.[2] Pāṇini enlists all such sounds under the caption *avyakte śabde.* Following is the list of such sounds enumerated by Pāṇini as *avyaktas.*

hra, na, ga, mla, ku, kṣa, va, kul, klaṣa, reṣa, hesṛ, hresṛ, sya, hikka, gu, siji

In fact, these sounds were located by Pāṇini in nature.

First origin of Action Sounds/*Ākhyātas*

The first and foremost origin of *ākhyātas* thus took place among the human-beings in the form of onomatopoetic utterances of monosyllabic or disyllabic nature, when they imitated natural sounds. A few examples may be cited which record this type of development in the early history of the origin of sounds. For instance, the following may be noticed:

---

1 *vācaṁ parjanyajinvitāṁ pra-maṇḍukā avādiṣu*

2 Pāṇini *sūtras* 5.4.57 and 6.1.98 clearly show that the term *avyakta* is employed to signify natural sounds.

	Physical action (Sounds in nature)	*Ākhyātas* (Physiological action)	To mean
1.	*'paṭpaṭ'* 'sound of falling rain'	√ *pat patane*	fall
		√ *pā pāne*	drink
		√ *paṭh vyaktāyāṁ vācī*	read
2.	*'caṭcaṭ'* 'sound of raindrops while falling on something'	√ *caṭ sphuṭ bhedane*	break in pieces
	(ii) wood breaking due to wind force.		
	(iii) green-wood burning due to fire.		
3.	*'tar'* 'sound produced by waters while falling continuously on earth.'	√ *tṛ plavan-santaraṇayoḥ*	float or swim
4.	'*kal-kal*' sound of flowing waters in the forms of rivers or rivulets.	√ *kalla avyakte śabde*	sound
		√*kal śabdasaṁkhyānayoḥ*	calculation
		and	
		√*kal gatau saṁkhyane ca*	movement
5.	'*hra*'	√ *hrād avyakte śabde*	happiness
6.	'*ga*'	√ *gā stutau*	Praise
7.	'*ku*'	√ *ku śabde*	sound

Second Origin of Action, or *Ākhyāta*/sounds

Second origin of sounds among human-beings took place in the form of onomatopoetic sounds uttered by them after imitation of animal sounds. Examples of this type of development may be given as under:

	Sounds produced by animals	Physiological actions or *ākhyātas* formed by human-being	To mean
1	*'bha-bha'* by cow 'bow-wow' by dogs	√ *bhasa bhartsana diptyoḥ*	Bully
		√ vad vyaktāyāṁ vāci	expressed sound
2	*'kha-khi'* by monkey to eat up enemy	√ *khai khādane*	Eat
3	'ra-ra' sound of dogs while scratching earth when in the mood of *fighting*.	√ *rd kṣobhane*	Angry
4	*'kra-kra'* sound of a crow.	√ *kāsṛ śabda kutsāyāṁ*	Unwanted sound.
5	*'dra-dhra'* utterance of pigs.	√ *drekṛ dhrekṛ śabdot-sāhayoḥ*	sound of encourage-ment
6	*'sarr-----r'* sound of flying birds.	√ *sar gatau*	Go
7	*'rava'* sound of bellowing cow	√ *rai śabde*	Sound
8	*'rabha'* bellowing sound by animals	√ *rabha rābhasye*	Bellow
9	*'cab'* sound of chewing by animals	√ *carb adane ca*	Eating
10	*'ghur---r'* sound of a flower bee	√ *ghūrṇa bhramaṇe*	Roaming

		√ *ghuṇa bhramaṇe*	
11	*'ku-ku'* utterance of a nightingale	√ *ku śabde*	Sound
12	*'gurr---r'* sound of a thundering cloud.	√ *garja śabde* √ *garda śabde*	Sound

Third Origin of action sounds/ākhyātas

Third origin of action sounds among human-beings takes place in their onomatopoetic utterances after the imitation of physical sound produced while doing some physical actions. This type of development may be traced to the following examples.

	Physical action	**sound produced**	***Ākhyāta* or Physiological action coined**	**To mean**
1.	beating	*taḍa*	√ *taḍi tāḍane*	Beat
2.	tasting	*tsa*	√ *ṣvad,* √ *svard,* √ *svādā svādane*	Taste
3.	fartening	*pard*	√ *pard kutsite śabde*	unwanted sound
4.	Walking	*paṭ-paṭ*	√ *pada gatau.,* √*pata gatu*	Go
5.	Watering	*car----r*	√ *kṣara kṣaraṇe* √ *sac secane*	leak or to water
6.	Breaking	*bhaṭ*	√ *bhidir avayave*	make parts
7.	Smelling	*sañ siñ*	√ *śighi āghrāṇe*	Smell
8.	taking a sip	*cuṣa*	√ *cūṣa pāne*	Drink
9.	Vomiting	*vu-vu*	√ *ṭuvam udgiraṇe*	Vomit
10	Hiccup	*hikk*	√ *hikka avyakte śabde*	Hiccup
11	Snoring	*ghra*	√ *ghra gandhopādāne*	Smell

12	sleeping	*si-si*	√ *śīṅ svapne*	sleep
13	discretory	*hat*	√ *hṛt puriṣotsarge*	discrete
14	eating	*ad*	√ *ada bhakṣaṇe*	eat
15	killing	*hin-hiṅ*	√ *hana hiṁsāgatyo*	kill
16	licking	*'lih'* or *'lap*	√ *lih āsvādane* √ *liṅ śleṣaṇe*	taste
17	shivering	*'I-I'* or *'vi-vi'*	√ *ira gatau kampane ca* √*I gatau* √ *ṭuvepṛ kampane*	go, shiver
18	breathing or filling air	*'sa-sa'*	√ *śvas prāṇane*	breathe
19	memorizing	*'I-I'*	√ *ik smaraṇe*	recall
20	weeping	*'ru-ru'*	√ *rudir aśruvimocane*	discharge tears
21	gleaning	*'mja-mja'*	√ *mṛjūṣa śuddhau*	clean
22	Accepting the idea	*'āḥ'*	√ *as bhuvi*	exist
23	sound produced by people while dividing something into two parts	*'huṅ'*	√ *huṅ apanayane*	divide or take away
24	utterance for shameful action	*'ha'*	√ *hri lajjāyām*	Shame
25	sound for	*'pā-pā*	√ *pṛ pālanapūraṇayoḥ*	Bring up

	bringing up child in arms			
26	sharpening	*'śāñ-śāñ*	√ *śān tejane*	Sharpen
27	Roast	*'bharr'*	√ *bhrasja pāke*	Roast
28	Drinking	*'gaṭ-gaṭ'*	√ *gaḍi vadanaikadeśe*	Swallow
			√ *gṛ nigaraṇe*	
29	Slip	*'sar---r'*	√*Āsraṁsu-avasraṁsane*	Slip
30	cleaving of logs	*'car---r*	√ *cara gatau*	go
			√*cṛti hiṁsāyām granthane ca*	kill and to knot
		'kar---r'	√ *kṛti chedane*	cleave
			√ *kṛñ hiṁsāyām*	kill
31	Hitting	*'caṭ-caṭ'*	√ *caṭ bhedane*	Hit
32	Kissing	*'cab;* or *'bac'*	√*cubi vaktrasaṁyoge*	Kiss
33	Spitting	*'sthu'*	√ *ṣṭhivu nirasane*	Spit
34	Sound produced by a person while resting	*'āḥ'*	√ *āsa upaveśane*	Sit
35	Arrow Shooting	*'as'*	√ *asu kṣepaṇe*	Shoot
36	Breaking	*'maṭ'*	√ *mus khaṇḍane*	break
		'bhaṭ'	√ *bhidir vidāraṇe*	break
			√ *bhidi avayave*	
37	Belching	*'dhra'*	√ *dhrai tṛptau*	Satisfy

Origin of Secondary *Ākhyātas*, or Action sound

All the above cited three kinds of utterances among human-beings may be regarded as the primary ones. Apart from the primitive action, roots of other actions or *ākhyātas* were derived from primary actions/*ākhyātas* on the basis of similarity of some meaning or sound. Such action sounds or verbs as derived form other primary verbs may be categorized as secondary ones. The origin of secondary verbs or actions may be assigned to various stages as per their origin from primary verbs or preceding secondary verb in chain.

An illustration of this type of development in the history of origin of action sounds of a speech may be made through a tree-diagram as under:

1.√ *Pā pāne*

↓

II. √ *piṅ pāne*

↓

III. √ *piḍa avagāhane*

↓

2. √ *Tṛ plavanasantaraṇayoḥ*

II

√ *tṛ taraṇe* | √ *tṛpa tṛptau prīṇane ca*

III √ *taraṇa gatau* | √ *tipṛ* √*tepṛ kṣaraqṇārthāḥ* √ *tuṣa pṛtau* √ *tepṛ kampane*

IV

√ *ṣṭpṛ* √ *stepṛ kṣraṇārthāḥ* √*thiipṛ*, √*thepṛ kṣaraṇārthāḥ*

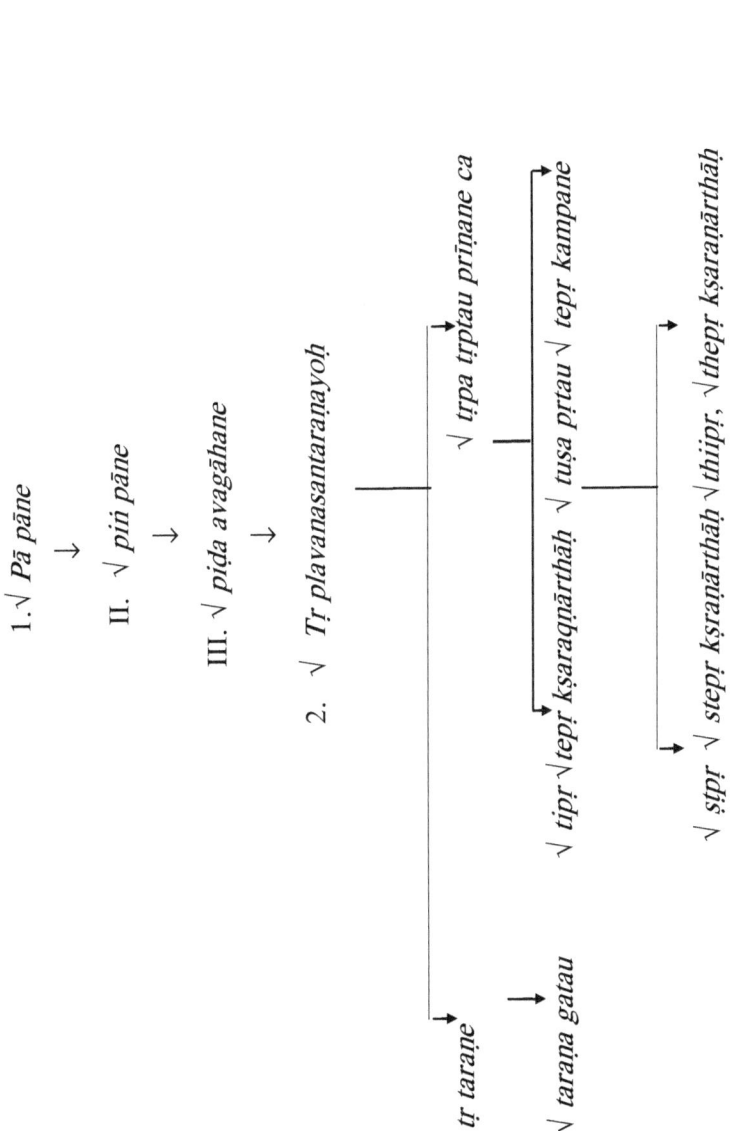

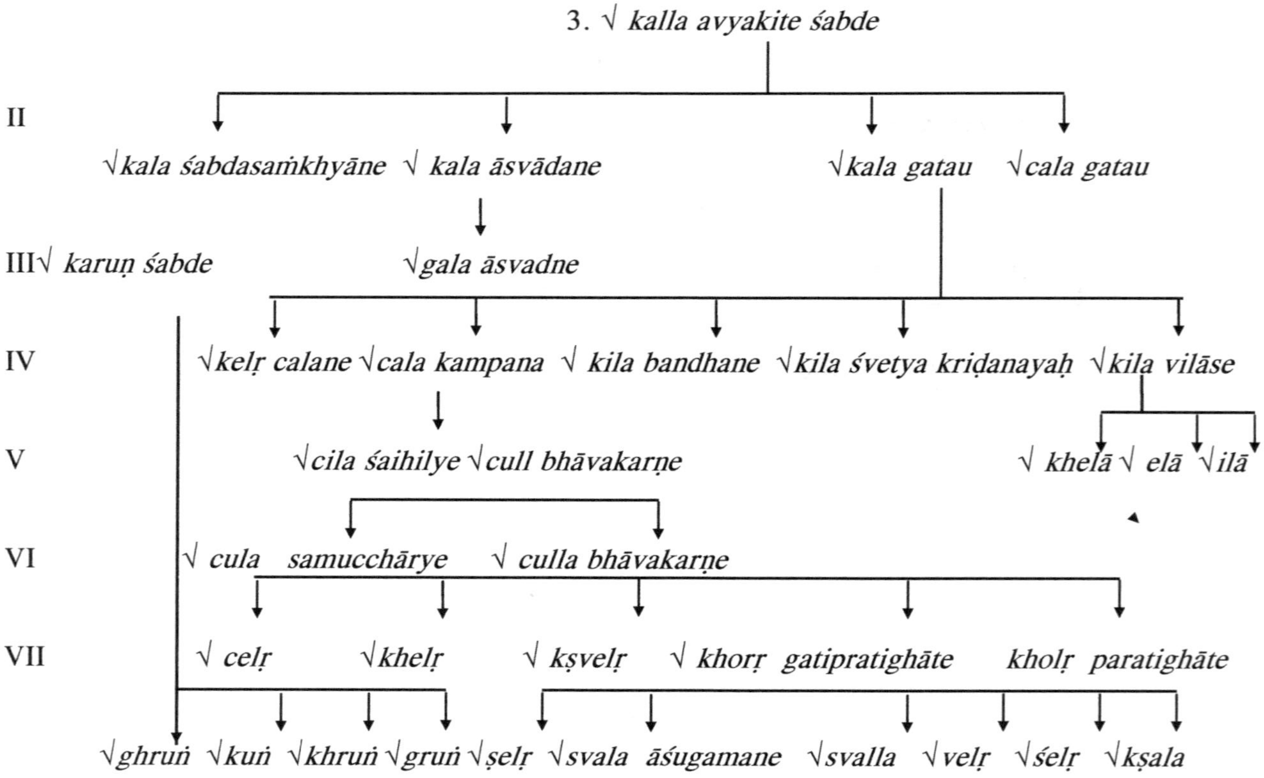
3. √ kalla avyakite śabde
II
√kala śabdasaṁkhyāne
√ kala āsvādane
√kala gatau
√cala gatau
III√ karuṇ śabde
√gala āsvadne
IV
√kelṛ calane
√cala kampana
√ kila bandhane
√kila śvetya kriḍanayaḥ
√kila vilāse
V
√cila śaihilye
√cull bhāvakarṇe
√ khelā
√ elā
√ilā
VI
√ cula samucchārye
√ culla bhāvakarṇe
VII
√ celṛ
√khelṛ
√ kṣvelṛ
√ khorṛ gatipratighāte
kholṛ paratighāte
√ghruṅ
√kuṅ
√khruṅ
√gruṅ
√ṣelṛ
√svala āśugamane
√svalla
√velṛ
√śelṛ
√kṣala

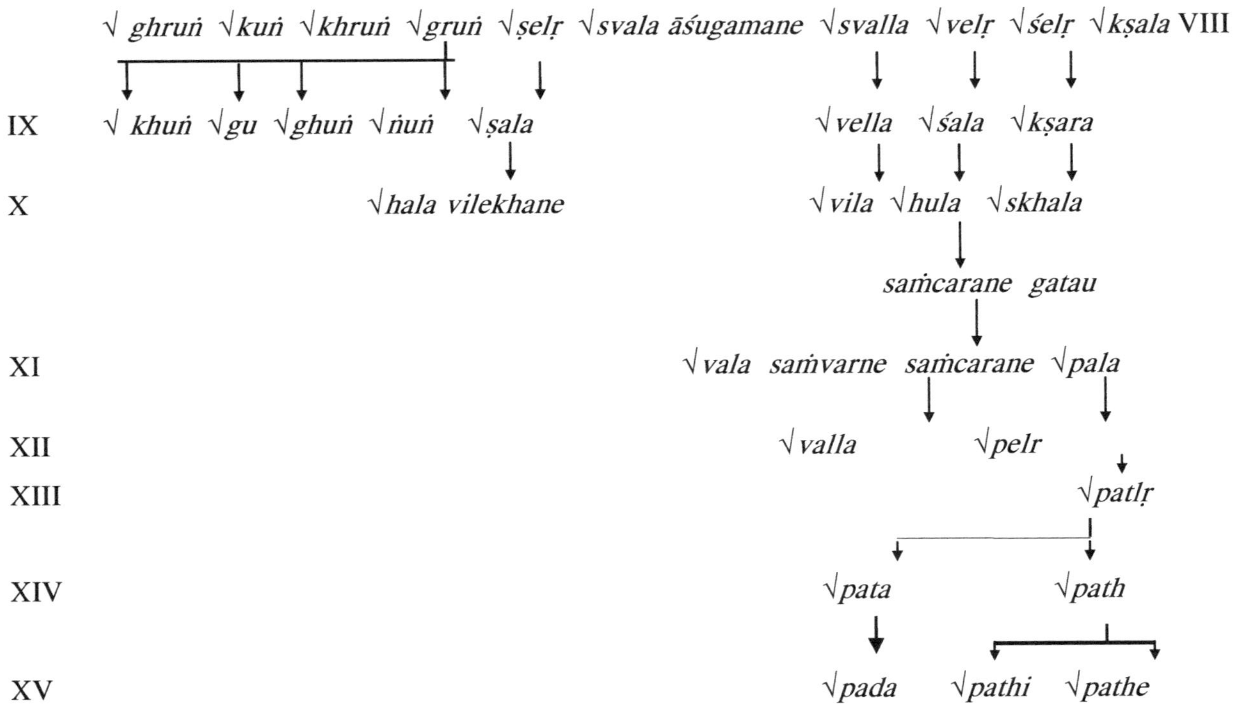
√ghruṅ √kuṅ √khruṅ √gruṅ √ṣelṛ √svala āśugamane √svalla √velṛ √śelṛ √kṣala VIII
IX √khuṅ √gu √ghuṅ √ṅuṅ √ṣala √vella √śala √kṣara
X √hala vilekhane √vila √hula √skhala
saṁcarane gatau
XI √vala saṁvarne saṁcarane √pala
XII √valla √pelr
XIII √patlṛ
XIV √pata √path
XV √pada √pathi √pathe

4 . √harad avyakte śabde

II	√hlādi sukhe	√kradi āhvāne rodane ca	
III	√graha kutsāyām	√kadi āhvāne rodane ca	√kladi āhvāne rodane
IV	√galha kutsāyām	√cadi ālhādane diptau ca	√klidi paridevane
V	√galbha dhārṣṭye		

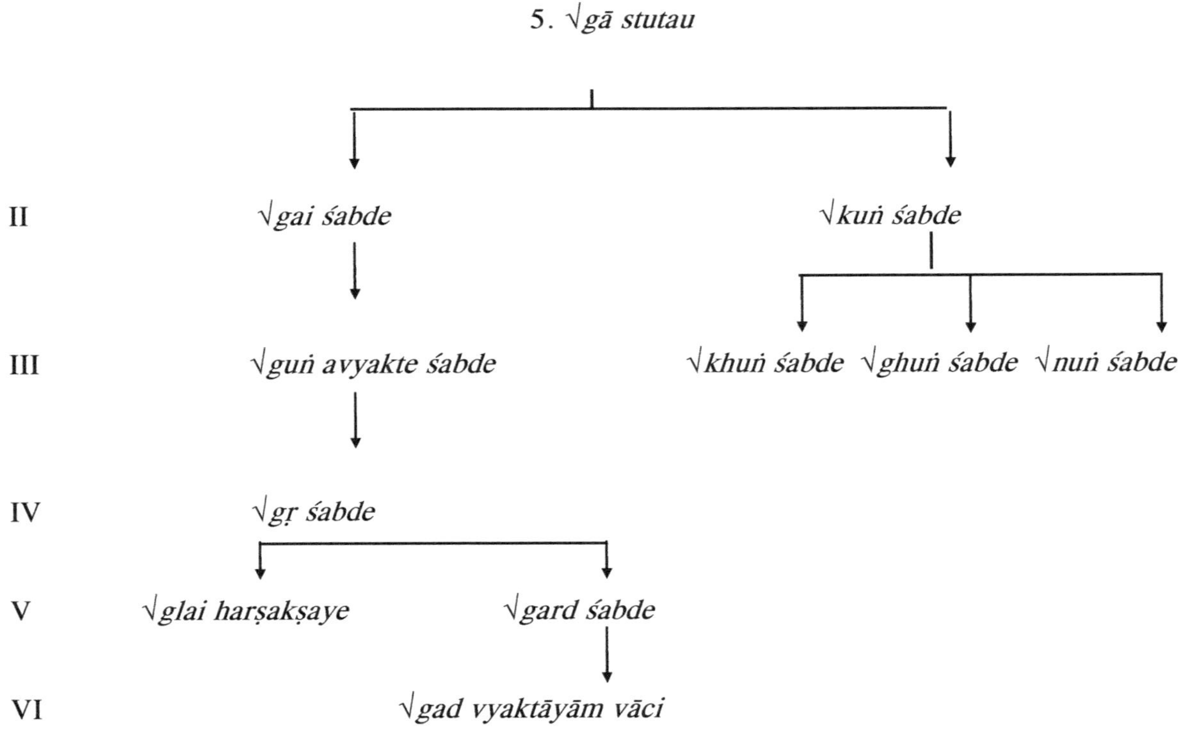

5. √gā stutau
II
√gai śabde
√kuṅ śabde
III
√guṅ avyakte śabde
√khuṅ śabde
√ghuṅ śabde
√nuṅ śabde
IV
√gṛ śabde
V
√glai harṣakṣaye
√gard śabde
VI
√gad vyaktāyām vāci

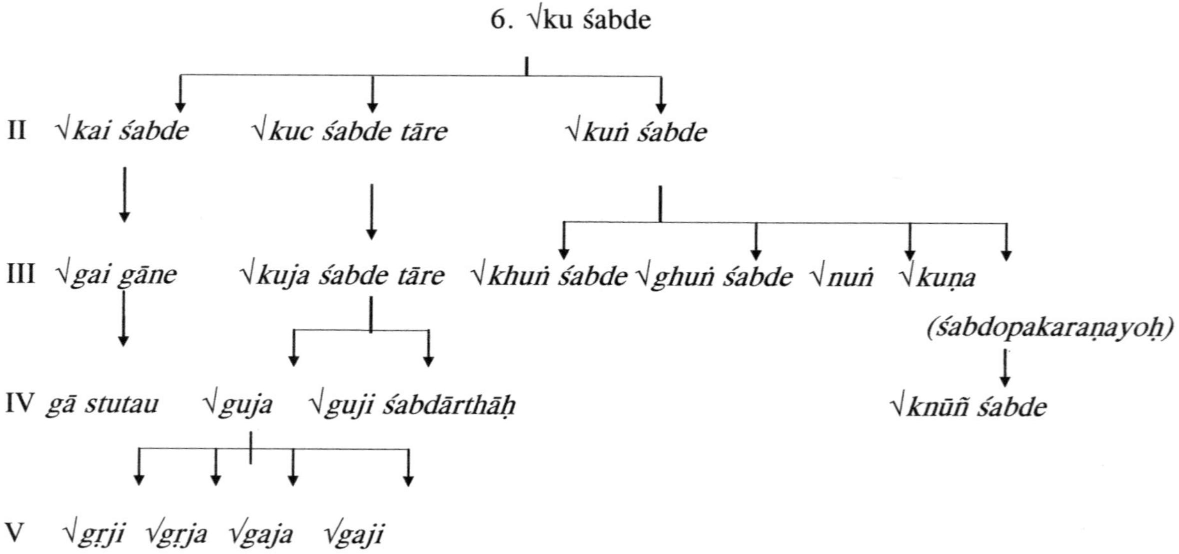
6. √ku śabde
II √kai śabde
√kuc śabde tāre
√kuṅ śabde
III √gai gāne
√kuja śabde tāre
√khuṅ śabde
√ghuṅ śabde
√nuṅ
√kuṇa
(śabdopakaraṇayoḥ)
IV gā stutau
√guja
√guji śabdārthāḥ
√knūñ śabde
V √gṛji
√gṛja
√gaja
√gaji

7. √*caṭ sphuṭ bhedane*

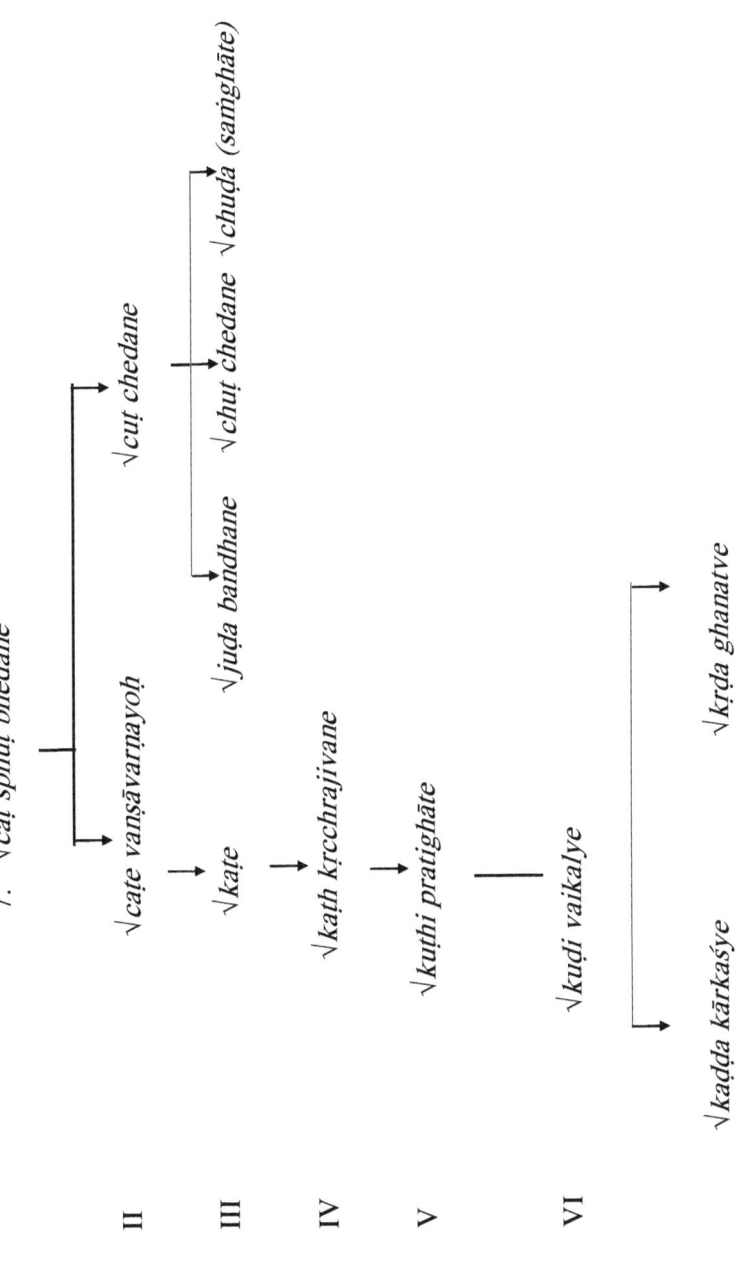

II √*caṭe vanṣāvarṇayoḥ* — √*cuṭ chedane*

III √*kaṭe* — √*juḍa bandhane* √*chuṭ chedane* √*chuḍa (saṁghāte)*

IV √*kaṭh kṛcchrajīvane*

V √*kuṭhi pratighāte*

VI √*kuḍi vaikalye*

√*kaḍḍa kārkaśye* — √*kṛḍa ghanatve*

8. *Vada vyaktāyām vācī*

II	√*vadiabhivādanastutyoḥ*	√*vaca paribhāṣaṇe*	√*vata paribhaṣaṇe*
III		√*bukka bhaṣaṇe*	
IV		√*bruñ byaktāyām vāci*	

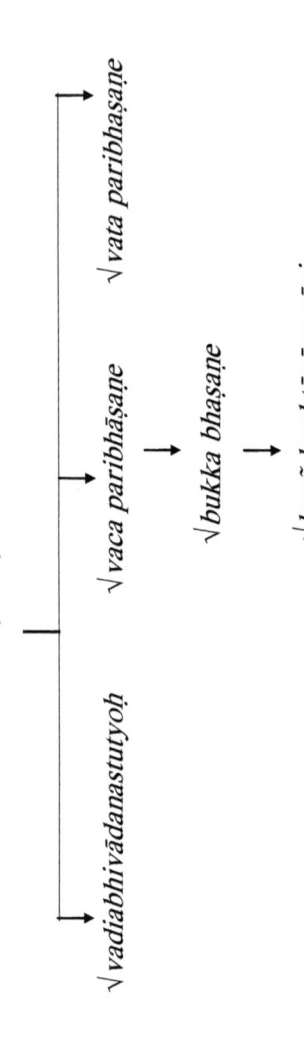

9. √*bhasa bhartsana diptyoḥ*

II √*bhaṣa bhartsane*

III √*bhrakṣa adane* | √*bhāṣa vyaktāyāṁ vāci* | √*bhaṭa paribhāṣaṇe*

√*bhāma krodhe* | *bhadi paribhāṣaṇe*

IV √*bhlakṣa adane* | √*bhakṣa adane* | √*plakṣa adane* | √*mlakṣa adane*

V √*bhala paribhāṣaṇa hīṁsādaneṣu* | √*bhalla paribhāṣaṇa ;hīṁsādaneṣu*

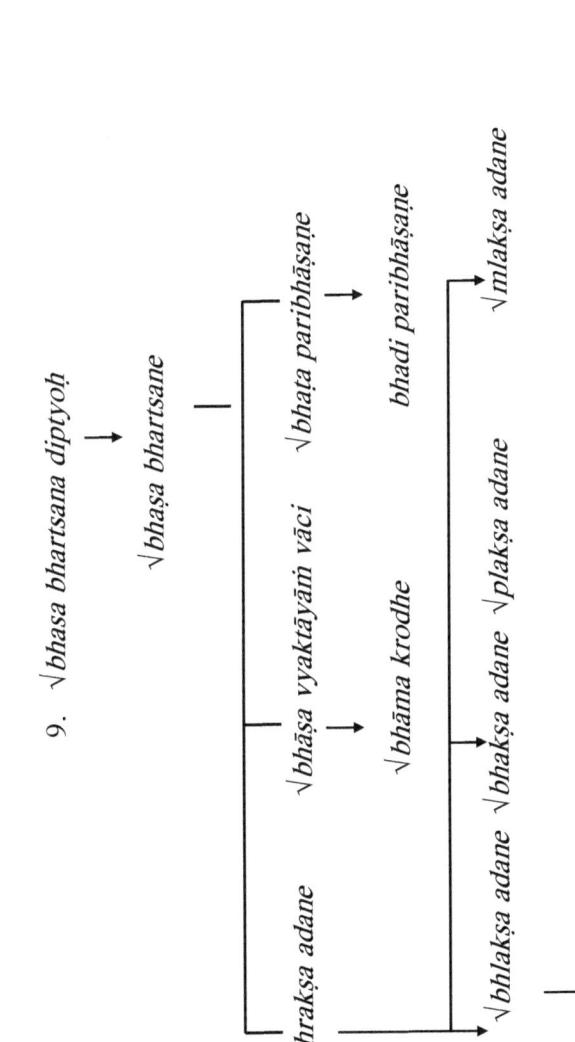

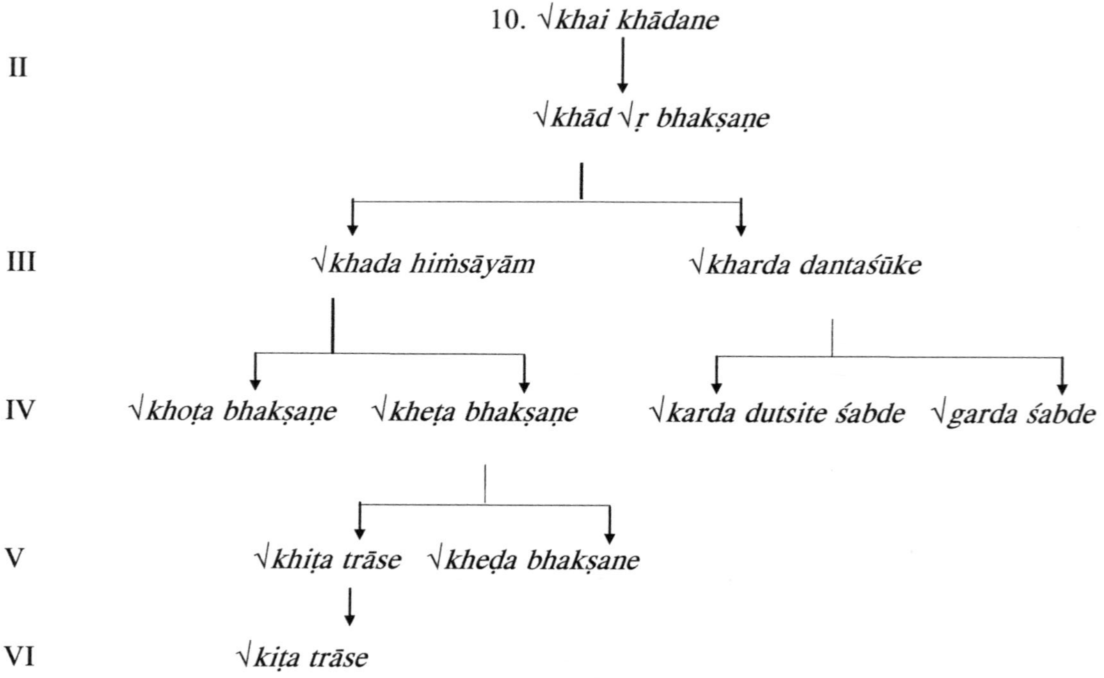
10. √khai khādane
II
√khād √ṛ bhakṣaṇe
III
√khada hiṁsāyām
√kharda dantaśūke
IV
√khoṭa bhakṣaṇe
√kheṭa bhakṣaṇe
√karda dutsite śabde
√garda śabde
V
√khiṭa trāse
√kheḍa bhakṣane
VI
√kiṭa trāse

	11. √*ṛd kṣobhane*
	↓
II	√*ṛdh bṛddhau*
	↓
III	√*radha hiṁsāsaṁrādhyoḥ*
	↓
IV	√*rādha saṁsiddhau*
	↓
V	√*rad vilekhane*

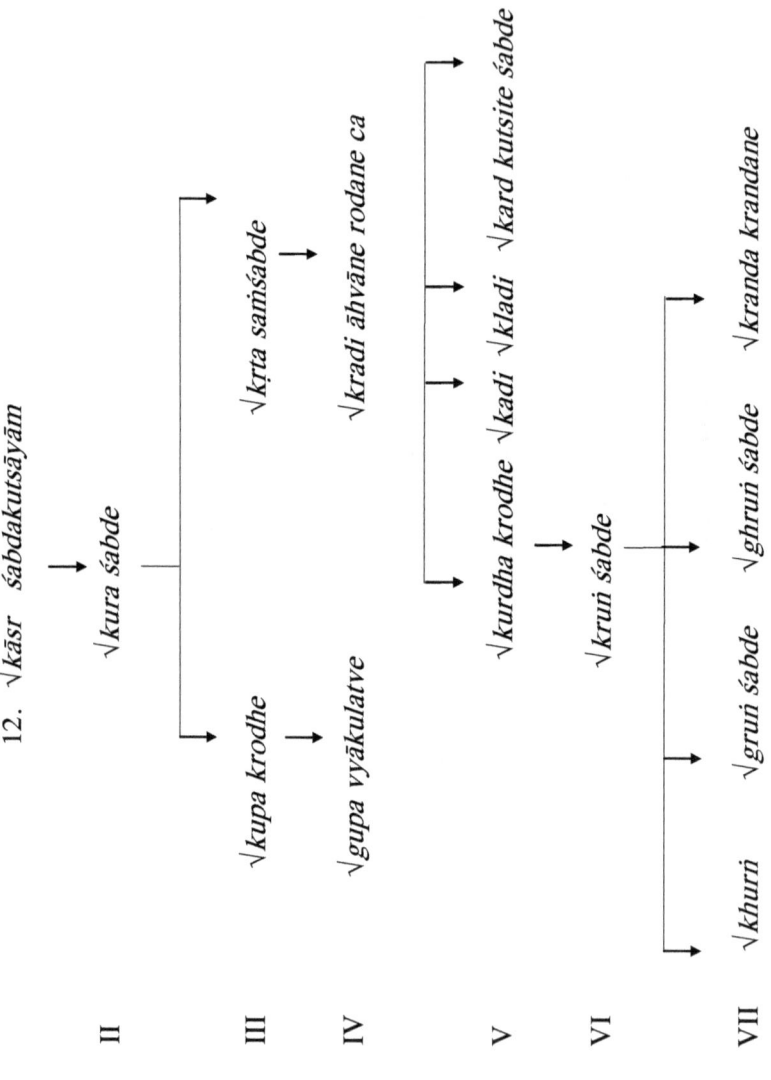

12. √*kāsr śabdakutsāyām*

II √*kura śabde*

III √*kupa krodhe* √*kṛta saṁśabde*

IV √*gupa vyākulatve* √*kradi āhvāne rodane ca*

V √*kurdha krodhe* √*kadi* √*kladi* √*kard kutsite śabde*

VI √*kruṅ śabde*

VII √*khurṅ* √*gruṅ śabde* √*ghruṅ śabde* √*kranda krandane*

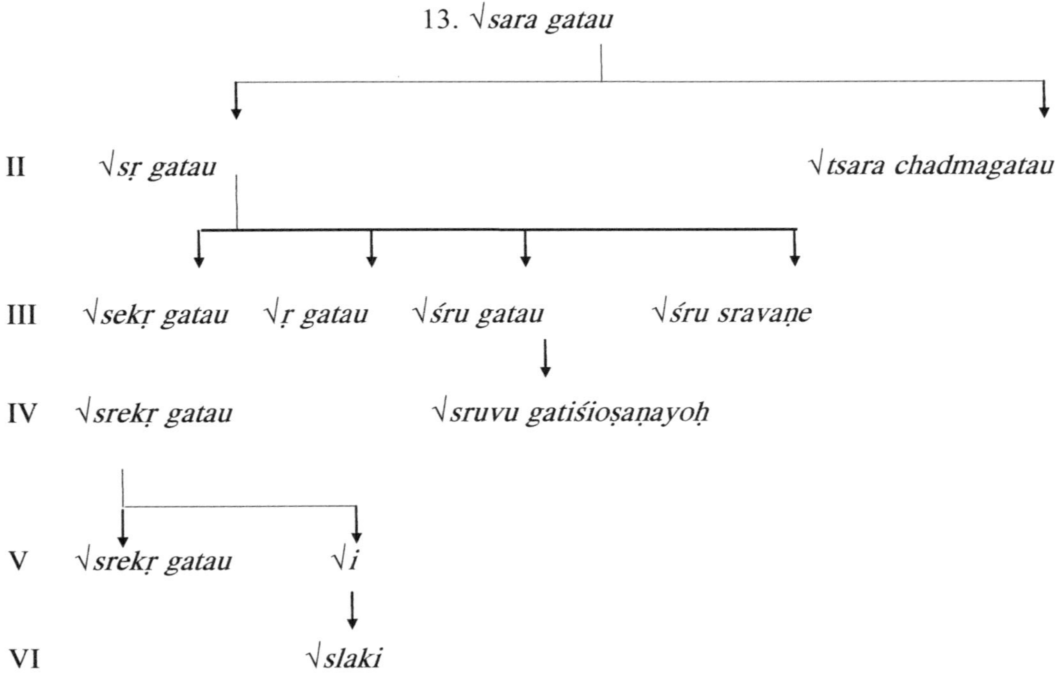
13. √sara gatau
II
√sṛ gatau
√tsara chadmagatau
III
√sekṛ gatau
√ṛ gatau
√śru gatau
√śru sravaṇe
IV
√srekṛ gatau
√sruvu gatiśioṣaṇayoḥ
V
√srekṛ gatau
√i
VI
√slaki

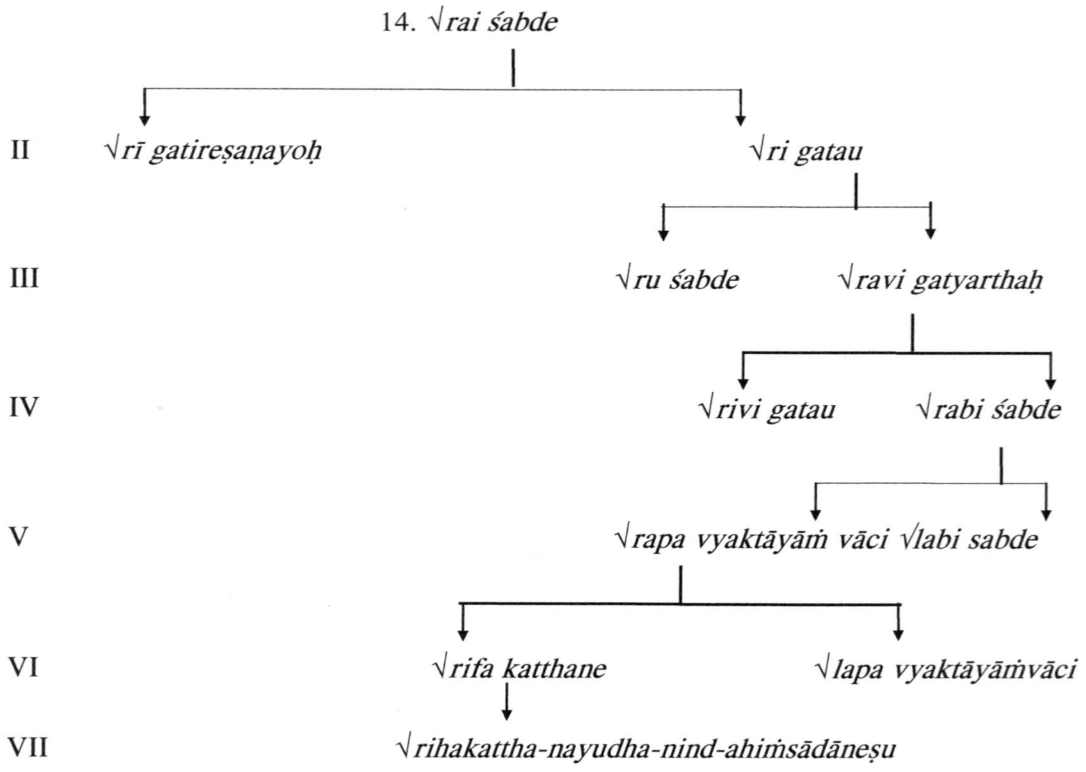
14. √rai śabde
II
√rī gatireṣaṇayoḥ
√ri gatau
III
√ru śabde
√ravi gatyarthaḥ
IV
√rivi gatau
√rabi śabde
V
√rapa vyaktāyāṁ vāci
√labi sabde
VI
√rifa katthane
√lapa vyaktāyāṁvāci
VII
√rihakattha-nayudha-nind-ahiṁsādāneṣu

VIII	√*riṣa*	√*riśa hiṁsāyām*
		↓
IX		√*raṭa paribhāṣaṇe*
		↓
X		√*raṭha paribhāṣaṇe*
		↓
XI		√*retṛ paribhāṣaṇe*

The above cited examples are suffice to understand the evolution of verbs/actions at the secondary stage. Thus all the verbs/actions were derived either primarily from some natural sounds or animal sounds, or sound produced while doing some physical action secondarily from the verbs/actions derived primarily from natural sounds, etc.

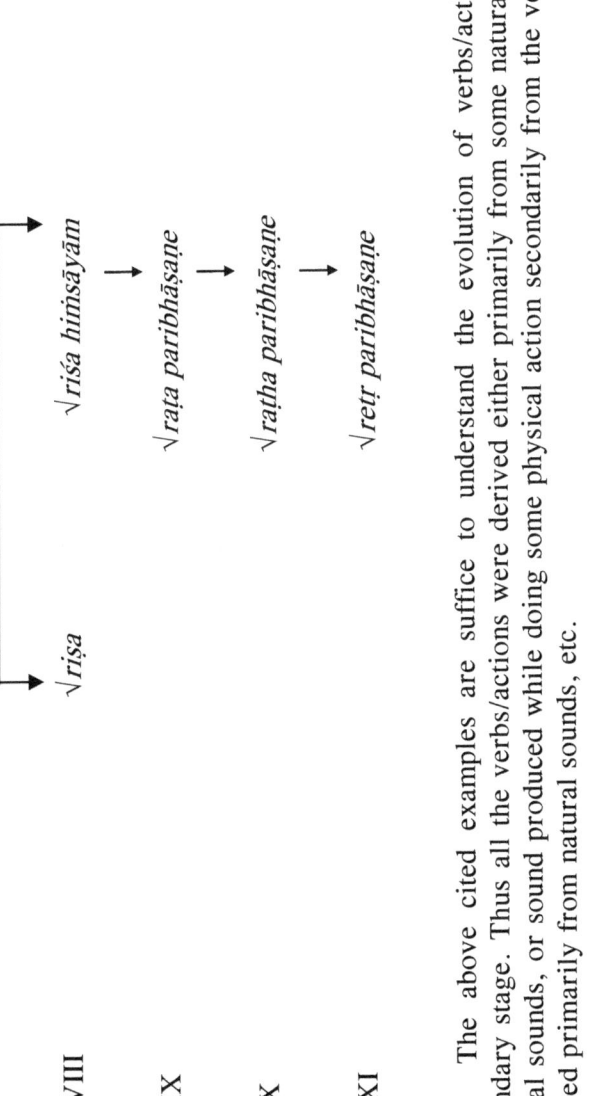

The above cited examples are suffice to understand the evolution of verbs/actions at the secondary stage. Thus all the verbs/actions were derived either primarily from some natural sounds or animal sounds, or sound produced while doing some physical action secondarily from the verbs/actions derived primarily from natural sounds, etc.

Origin of Names
(Agent Sounds)

After the derivation of large number of actions was over, various actions began to be associated permanently to the various objects or animals in the surrounding. Slowly and steadily the permanently associated actions became agents of their respective objects and animals and thenceforth the objects and animals began to be recognized with the help of their agents. The actions or action sounds thus transformed into agents were later came to be known as nāman or nouns. For instance Yāska (*Nirukta*, 1.10) observes in this regard as :

> 'The action that has fixed itself with some object or thing is associated with that object as its name or noun.'[1]

Similar are the observations of Śaunaka, the author of *Bṛhaddevatā.* He had it as :

> 'The actions that has become the agent of some object or thing is called *nāma* or noun.'[2]

For instance the action of *ādatte* i.e. taking or drawing (water-vapours) was associated to the object in the night sky (Sun). Hence in course of time, it became the agent of the object and was forthwith known as *āditya.*

Similarly, the action of *ahan* (non-killing) was associated with the animal cow, hence the agent sound produced for it was *aghanyā.*

> *aghanyā'hantavyā iti*[3]
>
> 'Cow is that which is not to be killed.'

Thus from the foregoing examples it can easily be inferred that all the agents, or names embody some action. That is why, the *Bṛhaddevatā* and *Nirukta* speak of involvement of actions into nouns or nouns as embodiment of actions, e.g.

---

[1] *mūrtaṁ sattvabhūtaṁ sattvanāmabhiḥ*

[2] *mūrtaṁ sattvabhūtaṁ bhāvaṁ nāmaśabdenābhidhīyate.*

[3] *Bṛhaddevatā,* 11.13

> 'Nouns are not without actions, so all the nouns are formed from some or other action.'[1]
>
> 'Nouns are born of actions.'[2]

The author of *Bṛhaddevatā* enumerates several such actions as are embodied in the names of Vedic deities or *laukika* objects or things, e.g. actions of residing, appearing, speaking or sounding, praying, living or abiding in close proximity were embodied in the names of various objects and things in the Vedic times. According to Śaunka (*Bṛhaddevatā*, 1.27;28) :

> 'All the names are formed from actions, this was the view of Śaunka. According to him, benediction and appearance are all expressed by action. The accident, residence and 'being the posterity of some one' are all actions. I'll let you know the reasons behind this.'[3]

In fact, all the above cited actions helped the early man to coin names of various objects in the natural surroundings. This fact also substantiate the idea that the Vedas were written first ever since the humanity arose from its primitive stage.

Attributives as the Prototypes of Nouns

The first development of nouns embodying some actions took place in the form of attributives/adjectives or qualifiers. The glaring examples in support of this historical fact, i.e. regarding the development of actions into attributive names can be located in earliest literary record of Vedic texts.

For instance, the action of *mitrava* 'roaring in measures' became the agent sound for winds, hence gets embodied in their name *maruta*. The name *maruta* first of all came to be used as attributive one. The *RV.* (1.182.2) records the attributive behaviour of the same as *maruttamā* where the agent sound

---

[1] *nānyatra bhāvānāmāni tasmāt sarvāṇi karmataḥ (Bṛhaddevtā, 1.31)*

[2] *namāni ākhyātajāni* (*Nirukta*, 1.4)

[3] *sarvāṇyetāni nāmāni karmatas tvāha Śaunkaḥ*
āśī rūpaṁ ca vācyaṁ sarvaṁ bhavati karmataḥ
yadṛchayopavasan āmuṣyāyaṇācca yat
tathā tadapi karmaiva tacchṛṇudhvaṁ ca hetavaḥ

marut partakes of the suffixes of comparison. This is also the pointer to the fact that till the time of *RV.* since its origin the embodied action (*mitrava*) remained alive in its agent, but by and by with the passage of time it (the embodied action) lost its colour, and receded to the background and so its attributive behaviour was also abandoned and it assumed the character of a proper noun. This is why, later Vedic and post Vedic texts are conspicuous with absence of its use as an attributive.

Similarly on account of the action of destroying clouds (*irāṁ dṛṇāti*), or passing into earth (*indau ramati*), or surging towards earth (*indave dravatīti vā*), or lightning the objects in darkness (*indhe bhūtāni*), electricity or lightning was called Indra. *RV.* attests its earliest attributive from as *indratama*[1]. The *VS.* (38.16), *Kān.* (38.3.2) and *MS.* (4.9.9) also register its attributive behaviour as *indratame*, but in the post Vedic literature it loses its embodied action and assumes the character of proper name.

During the course of my study, I have come across hundreds of such examples in the Vedas as are used as attributive names, but in the *Brāhmaṇas* the same attributive names have appeared as synonyms or alternate words.

For example, the word *bhānu* has occurred in the *Ṛgveda* (1.9.12) attributing *sūrya*, as in

bhānunā saṁ sūryeṇa rocase

But later on the same word becomes the synonym of *sūrya*. For more detail, see author (1991 :70).

Thus from the foregoing discussion, it is proved that all the proper names in their early stages of development have passed through the stage of their being attributive names.

If we describe the actions as fluids, adjectives will be semi-fluids and proper names/nouns will be the rigid ones. So the tendency or origin of human speech may be defined from fluid stage to the rigid stage. This is why, Yāska and other etymologists strived to locate the lost action while

---

1 *RV.* 1.112.8; 7.19.3

etymologizing Vedic vocables. In fact, they were attempting to search the fluid stage of the agents in rigid stage.

The main characteristic of the attributive sound in fluid stage is that an attributive can be used to several objects due to its fluidity, but, on the contrary, a rigid agent can only be used with one particular object.

To sum up, it can be maintained that so long as the action embodied in agent sound is alive, the agent sound is known as adjective or attributive name, but as soon as the action loses its colour and recedes to the background, the agent sound assumes the character of a proper noun.

Divine Origin of Speech

The first articulate speech consisting of action sounds, attributive names and proper names was in undefined form in the beginning. *Śatapatha Brāhmaṇa* (4.1.3.16) maintains that the articulate speech, or *vyakta/turīya vāk* spoken by men, animals, birds or creepers was in *nipāta* or undefined, (*anirukta*) form.

> 'The speech articulated either by men, or animals, or birds, or creepers, etc. is always unetymolized or undefined one.'[1]

Later on, Patañjali, the author of *Mahābhāṣya* (*Paspaśānhika*) substantiate the same view as :

> 'That of the four types or speech, i.e. *parā, paśyanti, madhyamā* and *vaikaharī*, the fourth form, i.e. *nipāta* form, or undefined form of the fourth type is spoken by men who don't know grammar at all.'[2]

Thus form the foregoing discussion, it is crystal clear that origin of speech first took place in the form of onomatopoetic utterances that were undefined.

For thousands of years together this type of speech remained in vogue. The *RV.* describes this type of speech as primitive articulate speech.

With the passage of time, scholars got together to discuss the issue of articulate speech at length. Many scholars emphasized the need to standardize the speech by way of defining it into the possible components of root and suffix sounds. References of this type of assembly of scholars are made in the *Saṁhitās* themselves. *TS.* (7.4.47) records the minutes of one of such assembly of scholars over the issue of

---

1 *tadetat turīyaṁ vāco' niruktam yat manuṣyā vadanti*
athaitat turīyaṁ vāco' niruktaṁ yat paśavo vadanti
athaitat turīyaṁ vācao'niruktaṁ yat vayānsi vadanti
athaitat turīyaṁ vāco'niruktaṁ yadidaṁ kṣudra-sarīsṛpaṁ vadanti.

2 *caturṇāṁ padajātānām ekaiksya caturatha bhāgaṁ*
manuṣyāḥ avaiyākaraṇāḥ vadanti.

defining the speech sounds into roots and suffixes. The records of *Saṁhitās* had it as :

> 'Previously speech was grammatically undefined. The scholars (*devāḥ*) got together and approached Indra to say that speech should be defined (into the components of roots and suffixes). Indra took this job in his hands.'[1]

Thus with the view to define the speech in terms of grammar, a big operation was carried out by scholars at collective level in typical Vedic terms as *Yajña*. It went on for thousands of years at stretch. We come across the pointed references of this type of effort put in by a long tradition of scholars. *Ṛgveda* (8.100.11) records this historical fact as:

> 'The scholars gave birth to a grammatically defined or scientifically standardized speech, i.e. a divine speech which was earlier spoken in many forms of dialects by the then common men in the society.'[2]

In fact, in typical Vedic term, *Devas* were none others, but the scholars well versed in the philology and other sciences. The *Brāhmaṇas* have clearly defined the term *Devas* as scholars. They have repeatedly said it as :

> 'The scholars are devas.'[3]

The language thus evolved by scholars/*devas* was also known as *daivī*.

Tāṇḍya Brāhmaṇa (5.7.1) also reflects ample good light on this fact as :

> 'Scholars defined the language grammatically or analysed the *naipātika* words (undefined) into the components of root+suffix.'[4]

The *RV.* (10.66.14 & 7.103.8) records the names of two classes of scholars who performed this job as *Vasiṣṭhās* and

---

1 *vāg vai purā vyākṛtā'vadat te devā indram abruvanni-māṁ no vācaṁ yākurvīta tām indro madhyato'vakramaya vyākarot, yadaindraṁ padaṁ tena vācaṁ kalpayanti vāghye vaindri.*

2 *daivim vācam ayajanta devāstāṁ viśvarūpāḥ paśavo vadanti*

3 *vidvāṁso vai devāḥ*

4 *devā vai vācaṁ vyabhajanta*

Somins.[1]

The greatest tradition of scholars that handled this massive work effectively was described in the *Ṛktantra Vyākaraṇa* as to have started by *Brahmā.*[2]

The first scholar to analyse the speech was Brahmā. He passed on this tradition to Bṛhaspati. In fact, he was named as Bṛhaspti, because of handling this vast and greatest work amicably.[3]

Bṛhaspati led this tradition which analysed the speech consisting of the various animal sounds.[4]

He spoke this to Indra[5] and Indra to Bharadvāja.[6]

Bharadvāja was the most genius among all the ṛṣis who were engaged in this work.[7]

His authority in linguistics was accepted by everyone. Pāṇini (7.2.63) also quotes his view with the address : *ṛto Bhāradvājasya.*

Bharadvāja passed on this tradition to other *ṛṣis* and *ṛṣis* to the succeeding scholars.

Thus the work to give origin to a divine speech (standardise speech) accomplished in the course of thousands of years by a long tradition of scholars well versed in linguistic science.

This is why, it was termed in explicit terms as :

---

1 *Vasiṣṭhas pitṛvat vācamakrat* (*RV.* 10.66.14)
Brahmaṇāsaḥ somino vācamakrat (*RV.* 7.103.8).

2 *Brahmā Bṛhaspataye provāca Bṛhaspatir-indrāya Indro Bhāradvājāya, Bhāradvājo ṛṣibhyaḥ ṛṣayo brāhmaṇebhyaḥ*

3 *vāg vai bṛhatī tasyā eṣa patis tasmādu Bṛhaspatiḥ*

4 *Bṛhaspati prathamaṁ vāco agraṁ yat prairayata nāmadhyeyaṁ dadhānāḥ.* (*RV.* 10.21.1).

5 *Bṛhaspatir-indrāya divyaṁ varṣa sahasraṁ śabda-pārāyaṇaṁ provāc.* (*Mahābhāṣya, Paspaśānhika*)

6 *Indro bhradvājāya* (*Aitareya Brāhmaṇa,* 2.2.4).

7 *Bharadvājo ha vā ṛṣīṇām anucānatamaḥ.* (*Aitareya Āraṇyaka,* 1.2.2)

saṁskṛtaṁ nāma daivī vāg-anvākhyātā maharṣibhiḥ.

> 'That is, Sanskrit is the name of a scientifically standardized language evolved by the seers out of the primitive articulate speech by subjecting it to grammatical analysis.'

In fact, this was not an easy job. The Vedic seers described it all like that of sieving grains with the help of a siever. The *Ṛgvedic* seer (10.71.2) had it as :

> 'The scholars sieved the language with great care and presence of mind, likewise the grain is sieved with the help of siever .'[1]

During the course of first operation/*yajña*, i.e. scientific standardization of language, the plethora of vocables of the spoken language was scrutinized and it was found that most of the words had evolved with a central sound prefixed or suffixed to some other sounds. The central sound was identified as an action sound and was taken as the root of the evolved word. So the entire language was defined into root+suffix or prefix combinations. Sounds preceding the central sound were defined as prefixes and sounds succeeding the central sound (root) were defined as suffixes. All such forms as could be defined on the above pattern were abandoned from the well defined language. However, some of the undefined forms were so vital to the life of newly structured language that they could not be dropped altogether. Hence, they were also permitted to form the structure of the standardised language. Since they remained undefined by the set grammatical rules, they were defined only as indeclinable or nipātas, *nipātanāt siddham.* (They are proved indeclinables). Pāṇini (6.3.109) reads this type of forms under *pṛṣodarādi* group (*gaṇa*) as *pṛṣodarādi yathopadiṣṭam* and accepts their validity as it is. Here the comments of Kaśikākāra may be taken into account. According to him, *pṛṣodarādini śabdarūpāṇi, yeṣu lopāgama varṇa vikārā śāstreṇa na vihitāḥ dṛśyante ca tāni yathopadiṣṭāni sādhūni bhavanti. yāni yathopadiṣṭāni śiṣṭair-uccāritāni prayuktāni*

---

[1] *saktumiva titaunā punanto yatra dhīrā manasā vācamakrata.*

tathaivānugantavyāni.

The words read in the *Pṛṣodarādi* class are not analysed grammatically. They were accepted as they were articulated by scholars without giving due regard to their grammatical analysis.

Origin of Vedas

When the first operation/*yajña*, i.e. standardization of language was over. The Devas, or scholars started second operation/*yajña*, i.e. operation chāndas, or documentation/composition of revealed knowledge with the help of first operation/*yajña*, i.e. standardized language. In this connection the Vedic seers themselves had it as:

> 'The scholars carried out the operation/*yajña* chāndas, i.e. composition of revealed knowledge (mantras) by means of the first operation/*yajña*, i.e. by means of standardized language. This documentation of revealed knowledge during the second operation/*yajña* was known as the first ever *Dharma* (literary compositions) in the literary history of humankind. The seers who documented this revealed knowledge were able to perfect linguistic expression to the actual intention of the earlier seers to whom this knowledge was revealed due to their appreciation of properties of the energy in light space (*nāka*). Those properties were also approved by the earlier *ṛṣis* who were having this knowledge by heart and did not documented it.'[1]

In fact, all the mysteries revealed to the seers regarding the creation were pronounced in the forms of literary couplets, or *Chandas*. Those couplets or *Chandas* were regarded as *Dharmas* (laws of creation). This is why, Yāska (*Nirukta*, 1.20), an ancient Indian Vedic scholar alludes to the Origin of Vedas (*Chandas*) as :

> 'There were *ṛṣis* to whom was revealed *Dharma* (laws of creation in the form of Veda *Mantras* or *Chandas*).'[2]

Thus the pronounces of various scientific truths or

---

[1] *yajñena yajñam-ayajanta devās-tāni*
dharmāṇi-prathamānyāsana
te ha nākam mahimānaḥ sacanta
yatra pūrve sādhyāḥ santi devāḥ.
(*Ṛgveda*, 1.164.50; 10.90.16; *Atharvaveda*, 7.5.1; *Vājasaneyī Saṁhitā*, 31.16; *Taittirīya Saṁhitā*, 3.5.11.5; *Taittirīya Āraṇyaka*, 3.2.7)

[2] *sākṣāt-kṛt-dharmāṇaḥ ṛṣayoḥ babhūvuḥ.*

mysteries in the form of *Mantras* or Chandas or literary couplets were known as *ṛṣis*.

> 'Ṛṣis were those to whom were revealed *Mantras*.'[1]

At another place it is explicitly described that

> 'Ṛṣi is the speaker of scientific truth, or a *Mantra*.'[2]

And the scientific truth revealed by him in the *Mantra* or the subject matter of his speech was known as *Devatā*.[3]

The records of Vedas tell us that the second great operation/*yajña* was not solely carried out or performed by one two or three ṛṣis or individual scholars, but collectively by all the scholars or ṛṣis. There number as per the extant recenstion of all the Vedas is 856. One of the seers of *Vājasaneyī Saṁhitā* (31.7) reflects an ample good light on this fact as :

> 'From the *yajña*, in which oblations were made by all *ṛṣis* originated *Ṛcas*, *Sāmans*, *Yajuṣas* and other *Chandas* (*Atharvaveda*).'[4]

In fact, in that great operation/*yajña* or composition of Chandas, no material oblation was offered, as usual, by ṛṣis. They made oblations in the form of pronouncement of literary couplets or Chandas. The pronouncement of *Ṛcas* was considered as the oblations of milk. Similarly composition of *Yajuṣas* worked as oblations of Ghee, and the composition of *Sāmans* was their oblation of *Soma*. This fact has very carefully been disclosed in the *Śatapatha Brāhmaṇa* (11.5.6.3,4,5).[5] Here it may be pointed out that the number of Ṛṣis to whom the knowledge of creation was revealed was only four, but the number of Ṛṣis who gave linguistic expression to the revealed

---

1 *ṛṣayoḥ vai mantra-draṣṭāraḥ*

2 *yasya vākyaṁ sa ṛṣī*

3 *yā tenocyate sā devatā.*

4 *tasmād yajñātsarvahutaḥ ṛcaḥ sāmāni jajñire.*
chandāṁsi jajñire tasmād yajus-tasmādajāyata.

5 *paya āhutayo ha vā etā devānāṁ yad ṛcaḥ*
ājyāhutayo ha vā etā devānāṁ yad yajuṁṣi.
somāhutayo ha vā etā devāmāṁ yat sāmāni.

knowledge was in hundreds. The *Mantras* in various Saṁhitās bears the name of composer Ṛṣis.

Classification of literary Couplets, or Chandas into *Ṛk, Yajuḥ,* and *Sāman*

As a result of the second great operation/*yajña*, a huge number of couplets/*Chandas* were composed by various enlightened ṛṣis on various aspects of scientific truths unravelled by their predecessors regarding metaphysical creation (consciousness) astrophysical creation (heavenly bodies) and physical creation which is present in the whole material creation/universe in three forms.

1. In latent form as energy or *Agni*, a dominating factor in the observer space.
2. In violent form as field (*Vāyu*) and electric force (*Indra*), a dominating factor in the intermediate space.
3. In ionized or luminous form as light (*Sūrya*), a dominating factor in the light space.

Thus the couplets pronounced regarding the latent form of physical matter, i.e. energy or *Agni* and its co-deities dominant in the observer space were christened as *Ṛcas*. The couplets produced on field (*Vāyu*), electric force (*Indra*) and their co-deities in intermediate space were named as *Yajuṣas* and the couplets dealing with light (*Sūrya*) and its co-deites in light space were called as *Sāmans*. The later Vedic scholars have alluded to this fact as under:

Śvetāśvatara Upaniṣada (6.18), *Aitareya Brāhmaṇa* (25.7) and *Manusmṛti* (1.23) had it as *:*

> 'To make the great operation/*yajña* a success, three types of (*brahma*) couplets were derived. From Agni (energy observer space) were derived *Ṛcas*; from *Vāyu* (field particle in intermediate space) *Yajuṣas* and from *Sūrya* (light in light space) *Sāmans*.[1]

---

1 *agni vāyu-ravibhyastu trayam brahma sanātanam*
dudoha yajña siddyarathaṁ ṛg-yajuḥ-sāma-lakṣaṇam

N.B. : Here *Brahma* means 'Veda' that is why, *Brahmacārī* is always known as who undertakes the study of Veda.

According to *Śatapatha Brāhmaṇa* (11.5.8.3)

> 'On account of three forms of energy (*tapta*) in three spaces, three Vedas or couplets of knowledge came into being. On account of *Agni* (energy in observer space) came into being couplets called *Ṛcas* or *Ṛgveda*, on account of *Vāyu* (field or electric force in intermediate space) came into being *Yajuṣas* or *Yajuveda* and on account of *Sūrya* (light in light space) came into being *Sāmaveda* or Sāmans.'[1]

On the basis of this classification of the knowledge, the Ṛṣis, to whom this knowledge was revealed, were also known as Agni, Vāyu, Āditya and Aṇgirā. Thus there were only four Ṛṣis to whom this knowledge was revealed. This revealed knowledge was documented in a literary form by the succeeding Ṛṣis. The number of succeeding Ṛṣis is around 856 as the records of extant Vedic Saṁhitas.

Authorship of the Vedas

There has long been a debate as to whether Vedas were created by God or man. It has always been answered : *vedāḥ apauruṣeyāḥ*, i.e. Vedas are not expressed by *Puruṣa* (some human being), but here the term *Puruṣa* has been taken up for both the meanings, i.e. for man as well as for God by the various contenders in order to support their contentions. Here it may be pointed out that the term Puruṣa here does not mean God but man. So the term '*vedāḥ apauruṣeyāḥ*' would only mean 'Vedas are not created by human-beings'.

The other way round also, the Veda being knowledge, or *dharma* would reside permanently in its *dharmī*, the object, the consciousness, or say consciousness being qualified by knowledge can be considered as its creator. Thus knowledge is the inherent quality of God.

---

1 *tebhyas-taptebhyas-trayo vedā ajāyanta*
agner-ṛgvedo vāyor yajur vedaḥ sūryāt-sāmavedaḥ [47]

Moreover it can again be proved on the evidences gathered from the Vedic literature. For example, the *Śatapatha Brāhmaṇa* (14.5.4.10) has made a clear cut statement that the Vedas are the expressions of creation. Accordingly :

> 'The couplets that are known as *Ṛgveda*, *Yajuveda*, *Sāmveda* and *Atharvaveda* are the exhalations of the created world.'[1]

At another place in the same work, it has been clearly picturized leaving no space for further doubt and suspense regarding the Godly origin of Vedas. According to the *Śatapatha Brāhmaṇa* (11.5.4.17) :

> 'There are two types of creations. One is the human creation produced through the sexual behaviour. Another is the divine or cosmic creation. *Chandas* deal with the cosmic creation. They are produced by *ṛṣis* through their mouth. Instead of sexual behaviour, they are produced verbally from mouth by *devas* or scholars to define the universal creation of God'.[2]

Thus from the forgoing discussion it can unhesitatingly be inferred that the couplets or Chandas revealed to various Vedic seers were the literary items originated first ever in the literary history of humankind. These chandas that dealt with the cosmic creation of God were pronounced by the ṛṣis through their mouth.

Here Gitā's views on Vedas may also be quoted. Gītā says : *triguṇaviṣayo vedaḥ,* i.e. the Vedas deal with the *triguṇātmaka prakṛti.* The material creation evolved out of the disharmony of three guṇas : *sattva*, *rajas* and *tamas.*

The above view and Gītā's view on Vedas clearly points out that Vedas are the knowledge of creation. And the creation

---

1 *evaṁ vā are'sya mahato bhūtasya niḥśvasitam-etad-va ṛegvedo yajurveda sāmaveda'tharvāṅgirasaḥ.*

2 *dvayāḥ vā imāḥ prajā daivyaścaiva mānuṣyaśca.tā vā imā mānusyaḥ prajāḥ mithunād prajāyante.chandāṁsi vai daivyaḥ prājās-tāni mukhato janayate tata etaṁ janayate.*

is the handy work of the almighty God. As such the knowledge of the Vedas can be called as the knowledge of the God and not the knowledge of a human being. For example, an engineer invents an engine; the knowledge of the engine is the knowledge of the engineer. A potter makes pot. Knowledge of the pot is the knowledge of the potter. Similarly, knowledge of the creation enshrined in the Vedas is the knowledge of the God.

Emergence of *Saṁhitā* literature

Later on keeping in view the huge number of scattered couplets on various aspects of scientific mysteries, it was decided to consolidate and compile the scattered couplets speaker - wise and subject-wise. Though earlier they were classified subject-wise as Ṛcas, Yajuṣas and Samans respectively but during the course of compilation they were again classified literary style-wise into *Ṛksaṁhitā Yājuṣa-saṁhitā*, and *Sāmasaṁhitā* respectively regrdless to their earlier classification. During the course of new classification, couplets composed on the style of prayers were compiled as *Ṛksaṁhitā* (*ṛgarcanī*). The couplets or Chandas composed in prose style were separately compiled in the name of *Yājuṣasaṁhitā* (*yat praśliṣṭaṁ paṭhitaṁ tat yajuḥ*) and the couplets attuned to music of cosmos were compiled under the caption *Sāmasaṁhitā*. (*gitiṣ u sāmākhyā*). The compilation of miscellaneous couplets came under the title *Atharvasaṁhitā*. So *Atharvasaṁhitā* became the representaive of all other three *Saṁhitās*.

Sequence of Evolution of Phonemes

The phonemes didn't evolve individually, but in course of formation of various words, various sounds evolved on account of combination of one sound with another. The question as to what the possible sequence of evolution of various sounds was or which of the sounds existed first to give rise to others to follow in a sequence was discussed and debated at length by the later Vedic scholiasts. Consequent upon which it was observed that *akāra* or *a*/*ā* sound originated first and all other sounds evolved from it when it was subjected to further vocalization, fricativization, breathing and mutation. In this regard, we may borrow from *Aitareya Āraṇyaka* (2.3.6) as :

> '*Akāra* or *a*/*ā* underlines the origin of all the sounds. It evolves into many other sounds when subjected to further vocalization, fricativization, breathing and mutation.'[1]

The sequence of origin and evolution of various speech sounds based on the analysis of various phonetic tendencies exhibited in the formation of various words and supported by ancient Indian linguists is rendered hereunder.

(1) **Sounds born first of all are = *a*, *ā***

Further vocalization led to the origin of following sounds in the second phase from *a* and *ā*.

(2) Sounds born from *a* and *ā* in the second phase

a*, *ā* > *e e.g. *rāma* + *bhyaḥ* > *rāmebhyaḥ*.[2]

Latin also exhibits the same tendency, e.g. Skt. *svasṛ* in Latin finds its change into swesor. Similarly, Skt. *vāyavaḥ* > Old Norse 'vestr', Dutch west.

***a*, *ā* > o** e.g. *sad* + *ta* > *soḍha*[1]

---

1 *ākāro vai sarvā vāk saiṣā sparśoṣmabhirvyajyamānā bahavī nānārūpā bhavati*

2 Pāṇini, 7.3.103

In Latin also Skt. *puruṣa* becomes pers<u>o</u>na;

P<u>a</u>ritātṛ > pr<u>o</u>tectus

ajr<u>a</u> > agr<u>o</u>

n<u>a</u>kta > n<u>o</u>ct, n<u>o</u>x

Sanskrit *n<u>a</u>kta* > Old Slav. n<u>o</u>sti > Old Norse n<u>o</u>'tt

a, ā > ai e.g. rām<u>a</u> = rām<u>ai</u>ḥ

Also in Gothic, Skt. *sabh<u>ā</u>* finds its evolution in h<u>ai</u>ms

a, ā > au e.g. *pap<u>ā</u>* + *a (ṇal) > pap<u>au</u>²*

a, ā > ī e.g. *putr<u>a</u> > putrīyati³*; *Pun<u>ā</u>* + *maḥ >*
punīmaḥ (we cleanse) *vāṣp<u>a</u>* + *karaṇa > vāspīkaraṇa*.

Also Skt. *vām<u>ā</u>* converts into old English w<u>i</u>fman;

Skt. *n<u>a</u>kta* > German N<u>i</u>cht > English N<u>i</u>ght.

a, ā is also elided e.g. *j<u>ag</u>am > atuḥ = jagmatuḥ⁴*

(3) In the third round further vocalization of the sounds evolved in the second round led to the origin of following sounds :

Form *i* evolves *u* e.g. *paṭhat<u>i</u> > paṭhat<u>u</u>⁵*

In Hindi also Skt. *k<u>i</u>ñcit > k<u>u</u>cha*

In *Mlecha* sounds recorded in the Veda, *h<u>i</u>ruk* becomes *h<u>u</u>ruk*.

In latest development of vernaculars also this type of phonetic tendency is visible, e.g. Skt. *rām<u>a</u>* changes into Hindi as *rām<u>u</u>*.

Similarly in the development of English also, the evolution of w<u>u</u>mman in Mid-English from w<u>i</u>mman of old English shows the same tendency of *i* undergoing the change of *u*.

i > y, e.g. Skt. *āt<u>i</u>* + *ācāra > at<u>y</u>ācāra¹*

---

[1] *ibid.* 6.3.112
[2] *ibid.* 7.1.34
[3] *ibid.* 7.4.33
[4] *ibid.* 6.4.98
[5] *ibid.* 3.4.86

Old Slav. *dvirī* > Old Norse *dyrr* (for door)

i > ***e***, e.g. Skt. root *ji* > *jetā*; Skt. root *ni* > *netā*[2] Similarly Skt. *plihan* > Latin splen and Greek splen. Similarly we find a change of Lithuanian no'sis > in to Old Frishian as nose.

i > **ai** e.g. Skt. *niti* > *naitika*; Skt. *dhri* > *dhairya*.

i > ***au***, e.g. Skt. *sakhi* > *sakhyau*; Skt. pati > *patyau*[3].

See also Skt. *īśāna* > Old Norse auster

i >***a***, ***ā***, e.g. Skt. *sakhi* > *sakhā* > *sakhāyau*. This type of tendency of change is also traceable in Latin and Greek where Skt. *pitṛ* finds its transmutation into pater. Also *i* of Skt. *duhitṛ* undergoes a change of *ā* in Greek thugater.

From *o* evolves *u*, e.g. Skt. *loka* > *luloka*[4]

go > *dvigu*[5]

Skt. *syona* > Old Slav. Suma

> Gothic Sūnna

> Old Frishian Sunne

> English sun

o> ***au***, e.g. *go* > *gau*[6]

Skt. horā > Gk. hōra > Mod. French heure > Old & Mid. English hour

o> ***ā***, e.g. Skt. *go* > *gām*[7]

śo > *śālā*

Skt. *no* > Avesta na > Old Eng. nā > Mid. Eng. na

Bāngru dialect of Haryana also have 'nā'

---

1 Pāṇini, 6.1.77
2 *ibid.* 1.1.3
3 *ibid.* 7.3.128
4 *ibid.* 7.4.59
5 *ibid.* 1.2.58
6 *ibid.* 7.2.115
7 *ibid.* 6.1.45

o> ai, e.g. Skt. *no* > *naiva*

o>a, e.g. Skt. *no* > *na*

bho> bhavān[1]

po > *pavan*

Latin octō, Gk. oktō >German acht, Mod. Eng. eight

Skt. *no* > Avesta na > Mid. Eng. na

From *au* > *u*, e.g. *atinu*[2]

Skt. *dvau* > Latin duo Greek duo > Mod. English two

au > ā, pau > pāvaka[3]

aṣṭau > aṣṭā, aṣṭa

dvau > dvā

Skt. dvau > Old Saxon twā > Old Frishian twā>

Old German zwā

au > o Examples of this phonetic tendency are discernible only in the development of extra Indian languages and Modern Indian vernaculars, e.g. Skt. dvau > Hindi - do

> Latin - duo

> Greek - duo

> Old Saxon - twō

> Old German - zwō

From e > ai, e.g. deva > daivika[4]

veda > vaidika

Skt. *ṛchate* > Greek regetai

Old Saxon Semīja > Lettish Saime

e > i sevā > siṣeve[1]

---

1 Pāṇini, 6.1.93
2 *ibid.* 1.2.47
3 *ibid.* 6.1.78
4 *ibid.* 7.2.117

Old Norse her > Old Saxon hir, her

Skt. *aphenam* > Latin opium, Gk. opion

e > a, ā deva[2]

śreyas > *śrāyas*

From ai > i *atiri*[3]

Avesta Haims > Latin civilis

ai* > *ā, e.g. *gai* > *gātā*[4]

mlai > *mlāna*

rai > *rābhyām*[5]

nai > *nāyaka*[6]

Thus it is obvious from the above discussion that sounds of u, y are produced for the first time and the origin of e, ai, au, a, ā sounds is repeated in this phase. Following sounds in this process complete their phonetic cycles, e.g.

a, ā > e > a, ā

i > a, ā > i

i > e >i

i > ai > i

ai > i > ai

a, ā > o > a, ā

a, ā > au > a, ā

(4) In the fourth round following sounds originated :

From u, ū > a, ā e.g. *bhū bhū* + a > *babhūva*[7]

---

1 Pāṇini, 7.4.59
2 *ibid.* 7.3.1
3 *ibid.* 1.2.47
4 *ibid.* 6.1.45
5 *ibid.* 7.2.85
6 *ibid.* 6.1.78
7 Pāṇini, 6.4.68

sphura > spharyati (6.1.54)

apagura + (*ṇamul*) > *apagāram*[1]

guriṣṭha > *gariṣṭha*[2]

bhuviṣṭha > *bhaviṣṭha*[3]

Also Skt. *manu* > Gothic 'manna'

Skt. *mūḍha* > Old Eng. 'mad'

u,ū > i, e.g. pū > *pipaviṣati*[4]

juhvā> jihvā

Cf. also Skt. *hanu* > Old Norse and Old Frishian kinni

u > ṛ, e.g. *kroṣṭu*> *krostṛ*[5]

Cf. also Skt. *sunu* Old Norse 'sunr', 'sonr'

u > v, e.g. *su* + *āgata* > *svāgata*[6]

Cf. also Skt. *vidhvā* > Gothic 'winduwo'

u > o, e.g. *bhuja* > *bhoga*[7]

ruja > *roga*

stu >*stotā*[8]

Cf. also Skt. *Sunu* > Old German 'Sunu' > German 'Sohn'. Similarly Old Eng. Sunu > Mod. Eng. Son

Skt. *udra* > Old Norse otr

u,ū > au, e.g. *guru* > *gaurava*[9]

muni > *mauna*

---

1 *Ibid.* 6.1.53
2 *Ibid.* 6.4.157
3 *Ibid.* 6.4.156
4 *Ibid.* 7.4.80
5 *Ibid.* 7.1.95
6 *Ibid.* 6.4.77
7 *Ibid.* 7.3.86
8 *Ibid.* 7.3.84
9 Pāṇini, 7.2.117

śuci > *śauca*

Skt. *guru* > Gothic 'kaurus'

Cf. also Skt. duhitṛ > Gothic 'dauhtra' and Eng. 'daughter'. Skt. mūṣa > German 'maus'

u > ai, e.g. *manu* > *manai* [1]

pūtakratu > *pūtakratai* [2]

Cf. Skt. *mūsa* > Mod. Dutch 'muis'.

No example is traceable in other Indo-European languages. Instead Skt. u seems to tend towards e in European language, e.g. Skt. *mukha* >Latin 'mentum'

But, no such phonetic tendency can be attested in Skt.

From y > i, e.g. *vyadh* + *ta* > viddha

y > v, e.g. *sfāya* > *sfāvayati* (7.3.41)

saryū >*sākha* (6.4.169)

In the fourth round newly evolved sounds are ṛ and v. Apart from these a, e, o, au, ai repeat their origin thrice. Following sounds complete their phonetic cycles

I. o > u >o

II. au > u >au

III. i > y >i

(5) Fifth round ends with the origin of following sounds form ṛ

From ṛ > a, e.g. *mātṛ* > *mātarau* [3]

vṛvṛte >*vavṛte*

Cf. also Skt. *vṛndaḥ* > Eng. 'band'

ṛ > i, e.g. *bhṛ* + *bhṛ* + *ti* >*bibharti* [4]

pṛ + *pṛ* + *ti* > *pipartti* [1]

---

1 *Ibid.* 4.1.38
2 *Ibid.* 4.1.36
3 Pāṇini, 7.4.66
4 *Ibid.* 7.4.76

No example form extra Indian or Modern Indian or Modern Indian vernaculars is traceable by the author.

ṛ > r, e.g. *dṛś* > *drakṣati*[2]

sṛj > *sraṣṭā*

mṛdu > *mradima*[3]

dātṛ + *ā* > *dātrā*[4]

No other example from I.E. or Indian is traceable so far by the author.

ṛ > ar, e.g. *kṛ* + *tavya* > *karttavya*[5]

sṛpa > *sarpa*[6]

vṛṣa > *varṣa*

Cf. also Skt. *duhitṛ* > Gothic 'dauhtar'

ṛ > ir, e.g. *kṛ* > *kirati*[7]

gṛ > *girati*

jṛ > *jīrṇa*

ṛ > ur, ūr, e.g. *pṛ* > *pūrṇa*, *pūrtti*[8]

ai + *mātṛ* > *dvaimātura*[9]

ṛ > u, e.g. *dātṛ* > *dātu*[10]

Cf. also Skt. *paritātṛ* >Latin 'Protectus'

Skt. *mṛd* > English mud

ṛ > ār, e.g. *kṛttikā* > *kārttika*[1]

---

1 *Ibid.* 7.4.77
2 *Ibid.* 6.1.58
3 *Ibid.* 6.4.161
4 *Ibid.* 6.1.77
5 *Ibid.* 7.3.84
6 *Ibid.* 7.3.86
7 *Ibid.* 7.1.100
8 Pāṇini, 7.1.102
9 *Ibid.* 4.1.115
10 *Ibid.* 6.1.111

vṛṣṇi > vārṣaneya'

pṛthā > pārtha

ṛ > ri, e.g. *kṛ* , *kriyā*[2]

mātṛ > *mātrīyati*[3]

Cf. also Skt. *ṛchate* > Latin 'rigit'

Skt. ṛṣi > Old French 'recercher' > English 'researcher'

Apart from the above cited cases, *ṛ* is also seen tending towards '*or*' (see Skt. *svasṛ* >Latin 'swesor'), 'er' (see Skt.*pitṛ* > Latin 'pater', Greek pater), 'air' (see Skt. *hṛt* > Gothic 'hairto', Skt. *stṛ* > Gothic 'strairno') 're' (see Skt. *kṛ* > Latin 'creare' > Eng. 'create; Skt. *ṛchate* > Greek 'regetai'), etc.

From v > u, e.g. *svap* + *ta* > *supta*

div > *dyubhyām*[4]

v > ū, e.g *div* > *dyūta*[5]

siv > *syūta*

Cf. also Skt. *dvau* > Latin duo, Greek dūo

Skt. *navam* > Gothic niun

v > au, e.g. *div* > *dyauḥ*[6]

Cf. also Skt. *vāyavaḥ* > French ouest

v > b, e.g. *vṛhati* > *bṛhati*

(*vabayora abhedaḥ* - *v* and *b* cannot be distinguished.

Cf. also Skt. *vṛndaḥ* > English 'band'

Skt. *vana* + *vas* > Old French 'baniss'

Thus by the end, as we see, of the fifth round (phase) ṛ

---

1 *Ibid.* 7.2.117
2 *Ibid.* 7.4.28
3 *Ibid.* 7.4.27
4 *Ibid.* 6.1.131
5 *Ibid.* 6.4.19
6 Pāṇini, 7.1.84

and b find their origin for the first time. The sounds a, i, au repeat their orign fourth time. Origin of u is repeated twice. Following sounds also complete their phonetic cycles.

1. u > v > u
2. u > ṛ > u

(6) Sixth round is marked by the transmutation of *r* sound into l. There is a saying among etymologists that *ralayorabhedaḥ* - i.e. *r* and *l* sounds cannot be distinguished. Examples are:

gir̲ati > *gil̲ati*[1]

par̲yaṅkaḥ > *pal̲yaṅkaḥ*[2]

R also survives voiceless breathing (:) as a result of its being dropped or silenced phonetically. Dropping of *r* sound and its survival as a voiceless breathing also finds its phonemic representation in Sanskrit as *Visarjanīya* (:), but in other languages, it is phonemically absent, as it is represented by its prototype (*r*) only, but phonetically it has been given due regard. English 'hour', 'father', 'mother', are examples of this type where '*r*' though phonemically retained, but phonetically loses its character leaving its remnants in the form of voiceless breathing. On the other hand, examples of Sanskrit voiceless breathing are :

punar̲ > *punaḥ̱* (cf. 8.3.15)

bālakar̲ > *bālakaḥ̱*

On the other hand, in this round we witness a transmutation of *ṛ* again in *r*. For example, nar̲ām occurs 16 times in *RV*. Its evolution into *nṛṇām* takes place in the Veda itself, which occurs 26 times in the *RV*. *Svasrām* (*RV.*) also later changes into *svasṛṇām*. Thus the phonetic cycle of *ṛ* > *r* > *ṛ* also completes in this round.

(7). In the seventh round voiceless breathing (:) or *Visarjanīya*, as it is called, give birth to the fricative 's'. Pāṇini has recorded

---

1 *Ibid.* 8.2.21
2 *Ibid.* 8.2.22

this phenomenon as : *visarjanīyasya saḥ*[1]

e.g. *rāmaḥ* >*rāmas*

(8). In the eighth round following sounds get originated from the dental fricative 's'

From **s > r**, e.g. *agnir, nirgamana, āvirbhāva*[2]

Skt. *rodas* > Anglo Saxon 'rodera',

Skt. *āyasam* > German 'eisen' >Eng. 'iron'

s > ṣ, e.g. *rāmeṣu*[3], *paṭhiṣyati, pariṣkāra*

s > ś, e.g. *nis* + *cala* > *niścala*[4]

haris + *candra* > *hariścandra*

Cf. also Skt. *sabhā* > Lettish śaime

s > t, e.g. *vatsyati*[5] , *acakāt*[6], *utthāna*[7]

s > d, e.g. *vidvadbhyām*[8]

Cf. also Skt. *hasta* > Gothic 'handus' > Old Norse 'hand' > Old Saxon 'hand'

s > n, e.g. *bālakān*[9]

Cf. also Skt. *puruṣa* > Latin 'persōna' > Old French 'persona', or 'personae' > Mid. Eng. 'personae' > Mod. Eng. 'person'

Cf. also Skt. *sabhā* > Gothic 'haims'

s > h, e.g. edhitāhe[10]

Skt, *soma* > Avesta 'haoma'

---

1 Pāṇini, 8.3.34
2 *Ibid.* 8.2.66
3 *Ibid.* 8.3.59
4 *Ibid.* 8.4.40
5 *Ibid.* 7.4.49
6 *Ibid.* 8.2.73
7 *Ibid.* 8.4.61
8 *Ibid.* 8.2.72
9 Pāṇini, 6.1.103
10 *Ibid.* 7.4.52

Skt. *vāsa* > German 'haus' > English 'house'

Skt. *sapta* > Greek 'hepta'

Skt. *saṣ* > Greek 'hex'

In this round '*r*' sound repeats its origin, whereas '*s*', '*ś*', '*t*', '*d*', '*n*' and '*h*' find their first origin.

It may also be noted here that some peculiar sounds of European languages such as '*x*', '*z*' and '*b*' also find their origin in this and next round from Indian fricatives. The origin of '*z*' may be illustrated through the following examples.

s > z, e.g. Skt. *sunu* > Mod. Dutch 'zoon'

Skt. *syona* >Mod. Dutch 'zon'

Skt. *svasṛ* > Mod. Dutch 'zuster'

(9). In the ninth round develops following sounds.

From ś > k, e.g. diś > dik[1]

Cf. also Skt. *daśam* > Greek 'deka'

From ṣ > k, e.g. *śuṣ* > *śokṣati*[2]; *dhṛṣ* > *dadhṛk*[3]; *kṛṣ* > > *karkṣati*

Cf. also Skt. *aṣṭau* > Latin 'octō', Greek, 'oktō'

From h > k, e.g. *vaha* + *syati* > *vakṣyati*[4]

voiced > voiceless voiced > voiceless

Cf. also Skt. *attaḥ* > Mod. French 'attique' > Eng. 'attic'

Skt. *duhitṛ* > Old Frishian 'dochter'

Where 'h' tends towards aspiration.

From **ś > ṣ**, e.g. *dṛś* + *ta* > *dṛṣṭa*[5], *naś* + *ta* > *naṣṭa*[1]

---

1 *Ibid.* 8.2.62
2 *Ibid.* 8.2.41
3 *Ibid.* 8.2.62
4 Pāṇini, 8.2.41
5 *Ibid.* 8.2.36

In addition, '*ś*' causes the origin of 'kh' and 'h' sounds in the European languages, e.g.

Skt. *śubha* > German 'hübsch, > Eng. 'handsome'

Skt. *kalaśaṁ* > Greek 'khvalikha'

From h > gh, e.g. *duh* + *ta* > *dughda*[2],

kāma dughā[3], *ghāta*[4]

voiced > voiced

We find in European languages Skt. 'h' tending towards inspiration, e.g. Skt. *duhitṛ* > Greek 'thugater' where 'h' evolves into 'g' instead of 'gh' But evolution of 'gh' from 'h' can be noticed within European languages itself, e.g. Old English 'dohtor' > Mod. Eng. 'daughter.'

From t > c, e.g. *utśiṣṭa* > *ucchiṣṭa*

Cf. also Skt. *sīdati* > Old Slav. 'sittian' > Mid Dutch 'sitten' > Mod. Dutch 'zitten.'

Here the change of 't' into 'z' is approximately the same type, though not literally the same.

From h > j, e.g. *han* > *jaghāna*[5]

hṛ > *jahāra*

Cf. also Skt. *hyas* > Old French 'geastram'

h > *jh*, e.g. *ac* + *hala* > *ajjhala*[6]

---

1 *Ibid.* 8.2.36
2 *Ibid.* 8.2.32
3 *Ibid.* 3.2.70
4 *Ibid.* 7.3.55
5 Pāṇini, 7.4.62
6 *Ibid.* 7.4.92

ś > j, e.g. *saj > sajjati*[1]

From ṣ > ch, e.g. *Iṣa > icchati*[2]

In European languages, in place of 'ch' and 'j', 'b' 'x' and 'z' sounds find their origin from Skt. 'ṣ' e.g.

ṣ > z : Skt. *swiṣṭa* > Old German 'swuozi'

Skt. *saṁgi* > Mod Dutch 'zingen'

ṣ > b : Skt. *swiṣṭa* > German 'siüb'

ṣ > x : Skt. *ukṣā* > German 'ochse' > Eng. 'ox'

Skt. *saṣ* > Latin 'sex'. Greek 'hex'

'g' also evolves in European languages from Skt. 'ṣ', e.g.

ṣ > g : Skt. *roṣa* > Greek 'orge' > German 'rasen' > Eng. 'rage'

Skt. *kalaśa* > Latin 'calathum'

From h > t, e.g. *āh + tha > āttha*[3]

h >d, e.g. *anaḍudbhyām*[4]

h > dh, e.g. *naddha*[5], *taddhita*, *uddhāra*

From t > th, e.g. *vathsara*[6]

Cf. also Skt. *mātṛ* > Old Irish 'māthir'

Skt. *trayas* > Gothic 'threis', 'thrija'

d >dh, e.g. *duh* + si > *dhokṣi*[7]

From ṣ > ṭ or ḍ, e.g. *ṣaṣ > ṣaṭ > ṣaḍbhyāma*[8]

---

1 *Ibid.* 8.4.54
2 *Ibid.* 7.3.77
3 *Ibid.* 8.2.35
4 *Ibid.* 8.2.72
5 *Ibid.* 8.2.34
6 *Vārttika* on Pāṇini, 8.4.48
7 *Ibid.* 8.2.57
8 *Ibid.* 8.2.39

From h > ḍh, e.g. *gūha >gūḍha*[1] *liha > līḍha*

h > p, e.g. *rohayati > ropayati*

h > bh, e.g. *ap + haraṇa > abharaṇa*[2]

Thus from the foregoing investigation, it is crystal clear that in this phase the sounds of '*k*', '*gh*', '*c*', '*ch*', '*j*', '*jh*', '*th*', '*d*', '*dh*', '*ṭ*', '*ḍ*', '*ḍh*', '*p*' and '*bh*' come in the limelight for the first time, while others like '*ṣ*' repeats their origin owing to cerebralization of '*ś*'. Some eccentric European sounds also emerge first time on the forum owing to their origin from Indian dental and palatal fricatives.

10. In 10th phase of development of sounds, all the nasal sounds get originated owing to the nasalisation of respective oral voiceless unaspirates sounds.[3]

Similarly all the oral voiceless sounds get originated owing to the aspiration of the respective oral voiceless unaspirates.[4]

In the process 'kh', 'ṭh', 'f' originated afresh, but 'th' and 'bh' repeat their origin. All the voiced unaspirates 'g', 'j', 'ḍ', 'd' also repeat their origin owing to the voicing of voiceless sounds, e.g. 'k', 'c', 'ṭ', and 'p' except 'b' appears on the scene for the first time[5]. European languages also exhibit the tendency tendency of Skt. 'p' undergoing the change of 'b' e.g.

Skt. *sapta* > Gothic 'sibun'

Skt. *āpnoti* > Latin 'obtenire' > Eng. 'obtain'

Skt. 't' is also found to have changed into 'd'

Skt. mātṛ > Old Saxon 'modar'. Old Frishion 'mōdar'.

In this round of development 'k' class sounds repeat their origin owing to the gutturalization of palatal class sounds,[6]

---

1 *Ibid.* 8.2.37
2 *Ibid.* 8.4.62
3 Cf. Pāṇini - *yaro'nunāsike'nunāsiko vā-* 8.4.45
4 Cf. Vārttika on Pāṇ. 8.4.48 - *cayo dvitīyāḥ śari pauṣkarasādeḥ.*
5 Pāṇini, 8.4.45
6 Cf. Pāṇini, *coḥ kuḥ* - 8.2.30

e.g. *paca > pakta.*

European languages also register this change while borrowing Skt. originals, e.g. Skt. *pañcan* > Latin 'quinque', Lithuanian 'penki'.

Palatal class sounds also repeat their origin owing to the reverse process, i.e.palatalization of guttural sounds,[1] e.g. *kṛ* > *camera.* Thus a phonetic cycle is completed as c > k > c

One more interesting development that took place in this phase was the de-aspiration of the voiced aspirate sounds.[2] i.e. from '*jh*', '*bh*', '*gh*', '*ḍh*', '*dh*', were originated '*j*', '*b*', '*g*', '*ḍ*', '*d*', sounds, egg. *śudha+ dhiḥ >shuddhiḥ; dugha+ dham > dugdham; yudha+dham >yuddham.*

As a result, '*g*', '*j*', '*ḍ*', '*d*', and '*b*' exhibit their origin other way round also, i.e. from '*jh*', '*bh*', '*gh*', '*ḍh*', '*dh*'. European languages also show sign of similar type of development, e.g. Skt. *bhrātṛ* > Velsh 'brawd', German 'brude', English 'brother' where '*bh*' changes into '*b*'.

Also voiced unaspirates, viz. '*g*', '*j*', '*ḍ*', '*d*' and '*b*' are aspirated and vice versa. (Cf. Pāṇ. *ekāco baśo bhaṣ jhaṣ antasya sdhvoḥ* - 8.2.37) giving rise back to '*gh*', '*jh*', '*bh*', '*ḍh*' and '*dh*' sounds, e.g. *budh + sa > bhutsa; duh > dhuk; budh > bhudbhyām ekaḥ.* Thus, phonetic cycle of following consonantal sounds is completed.

gh > g > gh

bh > b >bh

jh > j > jh

ḍh > ḍ > ḍh

In addition to this, we find that devoicing process of the voiced sounds like '*g*', '*d*', '*b*', '*j*', '*ḍ*', are changed into '*k*', '*t*', '*p*', '*c*', and '*ṭ*', e.g. *tad > tat*; *ud>ut*; *vāg>vāk; and ab> ap* (Pāṇ. *khari ca-* 8.4.55). (Note : Grimm's law is explained here). Similarly, reverse process takes place, e.g Skt. '*go*'

---

1 Pāṇini - *kuhośca* - 7.4.62

2 Cf. Pāṇ. *jhalāṁ jaśo'nte* - 8.2.39. Also *jhalām jaśa jhasi* - 8.4.52.

becomes ' c̱ow ' in English, '*ḏaśa*' becomes 'ṯen'and '*ḇādham*' becomes 'p̱ain'. (Note: This also explains amendments to Grassman's law).

Thus all the sounds developed in a long course of 10 rounds, or phases. Their origin and development may be depicted by a tree diagram as under:

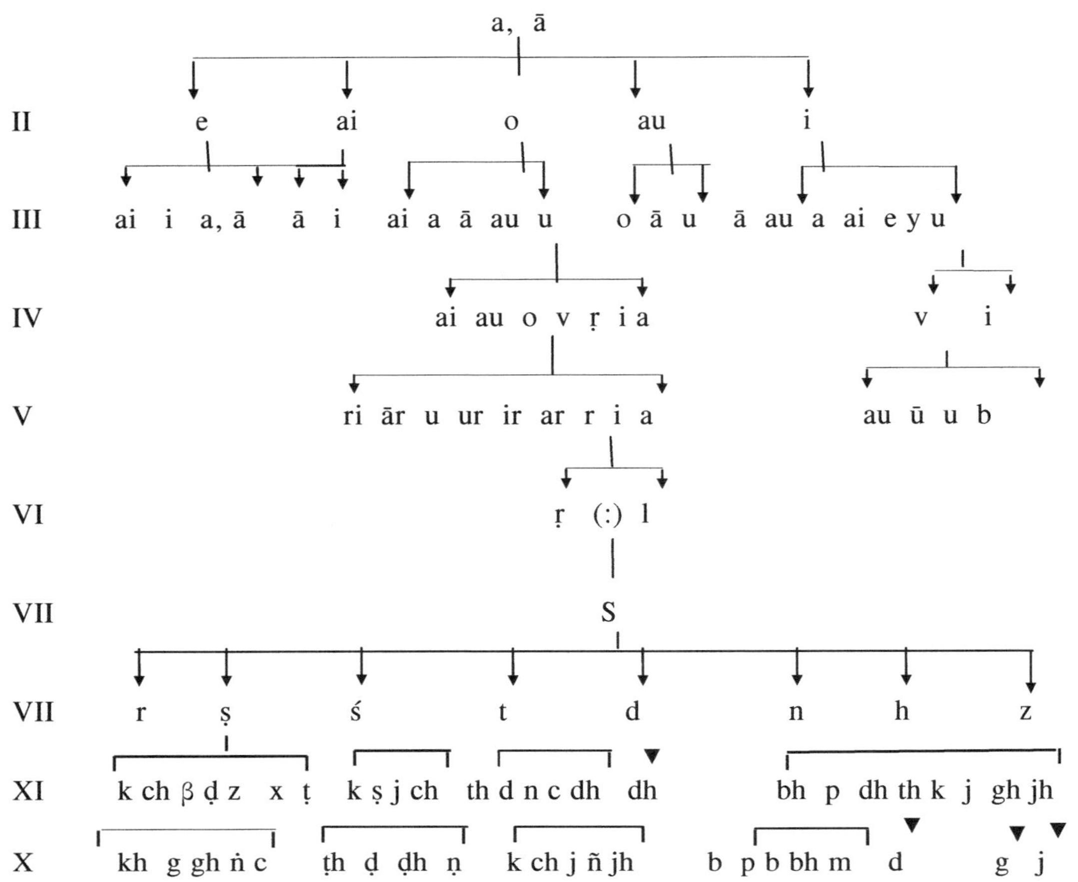
a, ā
II e ai o au i
III ai i a, ā ā i ai a ā au u o ā u ā au a ai e y u
IV ai au o v ṛ i a v i
V ri ār u ur ir ar r i a au ū u b
VI ṛ (:) l
VII S
VII r ṣ ś t d n h z
XI k ch β ḍ z x ṭ k ṣ j ch th d n c dh dh bh p dh th k j gh jh
X kh g gh ṅ c ṭh ḍ ḍh ṇ k ch j ñ jh b p b bh m d g j

Later on these sounds were defined phonetically and classified as per their place of articulation and articulator. They were divided into *svaras* and *vyañjanas* respectively keeping in view their role in the formation of words. *Svaras* were considered to be the prime-factors in the syllabication of words- *svayaṁ rājante iti svarāḥ* and *vyañjans* as marginal sounds going along with the *svaras* : *anvag bhavati vyañjanam.*

Origin and Evolution of European Languages

(A Phonological Analysis)

As already stated above, the standardization of speech by scholars (*dveas*) made it flow into two different streams. One among scholars as standardized one, another among laymen. The speech of laymen further underwent a change owing to further changed or renewed physiological, geographical and sociological factors. Here it may be pointed out that change is the law (particularly) of a laymen's speech, since it (laymen's speech) has no framed rules or laws to regulate its flow. Thus from the main-stream of the language of common men emerges a chain of sub-streams and sub-in streams owing to several factors of change. The mainstream and sub-steams borrow their diction directly from the mainstream and sub-in streams borrow their diction from concerned sub-streams thus indirectly/ traditionally owing its allegiance to the mainstream. The Vedic or Chāndas Skt. has never been the spoken language of common men. So it cannot though be taken as the prototype of the later evolved languages, but it can give an idea of the nature and type of the diction of the prototype i.e. the Vedic language spoken by common-men at that time, since the forms of common-men's speech were preserved in the Vedic language in their standardized form. Moreover different stages of the change at the *laukika* level also influenced the change at the Vedic (standardized) level. So different stages of change at *laukika* level may be understood from the different stages of Vedic language which are available to us.

This emergence of sub-streams and sub-in streams directly and indirectly form the mainstream and sub-streams was observed by a great Vedist and a philologist Swami Dayananda Sarawati as : 'Sanskrit is the root cause of all the languages. The languages like English found their origin or genesis traditionally or indirectly in it. One language corrupts from the other. For example English we originated from Sanskrit *vayam* on account of the vocalization of *vayam*. Similarly from *pitara*

(Sanskrit) came 'pater' (Latin) and 'Father' (English); form *yuyam* came 'you' and from ādim came 'adam' etc. This type of corruption is sometimes bound with certain rules and sometimes takes place accidentally. No explanation is needed to scholars in this regard.[1]

Now the question arises which are the sub-steams that originated from the mainstream with the direct borrowings of their diction from Sanskrit. Under the class of such languages fall Prakṛtas in India, Avesta in Iran and Latin, Greek, Old Slav, Lithuanian, Gothic, Old Norse, Old Saxon, Old Frishian, Slavic languages and Old Irish in Europe.

All these languages may be called sister languages or cognate languages, since they originated almost in or around the same time period from their mother Sanskrit. This fact may be strengthened on the basis of the forms borrowed by them from Sanskrit. For instance, Sanskrit '*s*' finds its transmutation into '*h*' in the corresponding passages of Avesta. For example, following uses may be noticed where Skt. '*s*' changes into '*h*' in the Avesta.

Sanskrit	**Avesta**
sā	hā 'they'
sapta	hapta 'seven'
sakṛt	hakeret 'once'
asi	ahi 'thou art'
asmai	ahmai 'to this'
svar 'heaven'	hvare 'sun'
sva	have 'his'

The similar tendency can be registered in abundance in the development of Prākṛta languages, where also the Sanskrit '*s*' changes into '*h*'.

It may also be pointed out here that the use of

---

[1] See Author (1991 : 73) : *Researches into Vedic and Linguistic Studies,*Granth Bharati Prakashan, Delhi, 1991.

periphrastic future is attested sparingly in the *Saṁhitās* and *Brāhmṇas*. It becomes more frequent in later literature. It is, as is well known, formed from the noun of agency by adding the verb substantive in the first and second persons. Avesta should also retain it on the analogy of later Sanskrit, a kind of the periphrastic future in which the forms of the third person were nomen-agentis inflected for the three numbers. Similarly, in the Avesta, the corresponding forms of the verb 'ab' are added to the noun of agency. In Sanskrit, we have *netāsmaḥ* (1st P. Plural) and *netāstha* (2nd P. Plural). Similarly in Avesta we have patamahi 'we shall protect'; patasto 'you will protect'.

To extend the ongoing discussion it may also be added here that the active past participle forms formed with the suffix-*vat* are peculiar to the later Sanskrit. Avesta also attests such forms as are identical with Sanskrit active past participle formed with the suffix-*vat,* e.g.

Root	**Past Passive Participle**	**Past Active Participle**
vûrû'to work'	varsta	varstavat
sā 'to become propitious'	sāna	sānavat

These example are sufficed to say that Avesta owes its origin to Sanskrit at much later stage other linguistic development.

A few examples, in case of principle languages of Europe can be quoted as under :

The Sanskrit infinitive, as is well known, has its wide ranging history from the Vedic period down to the classical one. The Vedic language attests the uses of over a dozen suffixes to convey the meaning of infinitive, but at a later period the use of other suffixes save *-tum* could not find the currency of usage. The use of Sanskrit infinitive suffix-tum is also recognized by the comparative philologists in the first part of the Lithuanian compound forms of subjunctive mood, namely 'dutumpbi', 'dutam-bei', 'dūtum-bime', 'dūtum-bite', 'dūtum-biwa', 'datum', etc. Thus, we can see the origin of other Indo-

European languages quite late from Sanskrit, as no other Vedic suffix except -*tum* survived in the later stages of Sanskrit seems to have percolated in them.

It may also be noted here that '*r* ' sound was more frequent in the times of the *Ṛgveda.* Later its use became less and less common and was replaced by '*I* '. The similar trend is discernible in the development of European languages. In those languages also the Sanskrit '*r* ' when followed by a dental occlusive ('*t*', '*th*', '*d*', '*dh*') or fricative (s) was sometimes replaced by '*I* '. For example, the Sanskrit form *jartu,* which is a side form of *jaṭhara,* finds its evolution in Gothic 'kilther', which is generally associated with Sanskrit *jaṭhara* replacing '*r*' by '*I* ' by comparative philologists. Similarly, the Sanskrit kar (s)u finds its development in the Greek 'telson', where too, '*r*' paves way to '*I* '.

Moreover, the active endings in the first person plural in the *RV.* have been-masi and -mas, former being more than five times as frequent as the later in AV. -mas becomes commoner than -*masi* and in classical language -*masi* disappears altogether. On the other hand, -*mas,* too, percolates in the European languages with little phonetic variations as -'mes' in Greek,- 'mis' in Latin, -'mes' in Old High German, -'me' in 'Lithuanian and -'m' in Old Slav. Examples to this effect are :

Sanskrit	*tiṣṭhāmasi, tiṣṭhāmas*
Greek	istames
Latin	stamus
Old High German	stames
Lithuanian	stowime
Old Slav.	stöim

There example also prove the fact that origin of the Principle European languages also took place from Sanskrit when it crossed the boundaries of Vedic phase.

Moreover, a comparative philologist Bopp, F. was surprised to see a remarkable concurrence of Prākṛt with Old high German and Latin in the point that both the European languages have contracted Sanskrit affix-mānayāmi, Prākṛta '-māṇemi', Old High German 'Var -mānem' 'I desire' and Latin 'moneo'.

Thus from the foregoing brief discussion, it can be observed that Avesta in Iran, Prakṛtas in India and Principal European languages owe their origin form spoken Sanskrit dialects almost in or around the same time period.

Moreover, it is also obvious that all these languages have originated directly from the language of Sanskrit speaking people, since all these languages exhibits the first change of phase while borrowing vocables from their parent language. For instance, during the first change of phase '*ṛ*' would appear, as maintained above, as '*ri*', '*ar*', '*u*', '*ir*', '*er*', '*r*', '*I*' and '*a*'. This tendency of phonetic change of first phase may be attested in the following examples of cognate Indo-European languages (identified by the present author), e.g.

Skt. *bhrātṛṇām* changes into Latin as 'Frātr-um'

where ṛ > u

Avesta as 'brathrāṅn'

where ṛ > r

Skt. *pitṛṇām* > Ardha Māgadhī Prākṛt as 'piuṇam'

where ṛ > u

Skt. mātṛṇām > Ardha Māgadhī Prākṛt as'māiṇam'

where ṛ > I

Similarly during first change of phase 'o' would undergo the change of 'u', the same may be seen in case of following examples

Skt.	>	**Avesta**	>	**Latin**
vas	>	vo	>	vos

The traditional origin of European languages with the direct and indirect borrowing from Sanskrit may be illustrated by the following example. Sanskrit *mātṛ* was borrowed firstly/directly by Old Norse as 'mooir,by Old Saxon as 'modar', by Old Frishian as 'modar', Old Irish as 'māthir' bound with the rules of phonetic change of 'a' into 'o' in case of Old Norse; of 'ṛ' into 'ir' and 'ar' in case of Old Saxon, Old Frishian and Old Irsh respectively; of 't' into 'th' and 'd' in case of Old Irish and Old Frishian and also Old Saxon.

The second phased borrowing of *mātṛ* took place into Mod. Dutch as 'moeder' via Old Saxon and Old Frishian 'modar' bound with the rule of phonetic change of a into e.

Its third phased borrowing may be witnessed in the Old German term 'moutar' via Mod. Dutch 'moeder' owing to the phonetic change of e into a thus completing a phonetic cycle of a > e > a in the above cited examples.

mātṛ > modar > moeder > muotar

The fourth phased borrowing took place in Mod. German 'mutter' via Old German 'muotar' owing to the phonetic change of 'a' into 'e' thus completing bicycle of phonetic change as a> e> a > e in the above cited examples.

mātṛ > modar > moeder > moutar > mutter

a > e > ā > e

cycle bicycle

The fifth phased borrowing seems to have occurred in Old English 'modor' via Mod. German 'mutter' owing to the change of u > o, e, > o and t into d.

Sixth phased borrowing may be attested in Mod. English 'mother' via Old English 'modor' with change of 'o' into 'e', thus completing a phonetic cycle e > o > e in the examples mutter > modor > mother

Here it may be observed that by the end of sixth round of indirect borrowing, a new phonetic tendency developed, i.e. the change of e > o > e which could not be registered in the earlier phases.

Origin and Evolution of European Languages

(A Morphological Analysis)

All the languages of the world have an interesting and long history of their origin and development. All of them have stemmed from their original source, Sanskrit (Vedic Sanskrit) just like various off-shoots of a tree. Some of them are directly associated with their origin and so they are easily cognizable and decipherable. Some of them, having passed through labyrinthine process of their development, indirectly and traditionally find their association with the novel inhabitants and having influenced by their new physiological, geographical and sociological backgrounds lost their originality and assumed altogether a new distinct form thus giving rise to a new family or class of languages. Nevertheless, in a way or other they have also evolved from one common source *i.e.* Sanskrit (Vedic Sanskrit). It is true what Maharshi Dayananda Sarasvati once observed "Therefore the Veda was expressed in Sanskrit, which is not the language of any particular region of the globe and the Vedic Language is the root cause of all other languages of the world"[1]

"Sanskrit is the root cause of all the languages"[2]

Most of the European scholars could not help praise the wonderful and copious structure of Sanskrit language. William Jones pronounced the Sanskrit language to be 'of a wonderful structure, more perfect than the Greek, more copious than the latin, and more exquisitely refined than either.'(*Asiatic Researches*, Vol. 1, p. 422). Prof. Bopp (*Edinborough Review*, Vol, XXXIII, p. 43) also had to confess that 'Sanskrit is more perfect and copious than the Greek and the Latin and more

---

1. इसलिए संस्कृत में ही वेद का प्रकाश किया जो किसी देश की भाषा नहीं और वेद भाषा अन्य भाषाओं का कारण है। =See Bharatiya, V.S. 2042 : 28-29

2 *Satyārtha Prakāsa, Chapter* 7.

exquisite and eloquent than either. Prof. Max Mueller (*Science of Language*, p.203) had to declare Sanskrit '*Language of languages*'. He remarked that 'It has been truly said that Sanskrit is to the science of language what Mathematics is to Astronomy.' Prof. Heeren (*Historical Researches*, Vl.XXXIII, p.43) recalls Sanskrit 'to be one of the richest and most refined of any. It has, moreover, reached a high degree of cultivation, and the richness of its philosophy is no way inferior to its poetic beauties, as it presents us with an abundance of technical terms to express the most abstract ideas.' Inspite of all their praises the western scholars, linguists or philologists were reluctant to accept Sanskrit as the original source of all languages. To hide this fact, they advanced their own surmises and developed a new idea of the existence of Proto-Indo European language which is held as common source of all Indo-European languages. This idea is merely based on supposition and have no confirmed or valid footing behind it and as such no genuine researcher who has troubled his head a little bit in this direction cannot hold this baseless and false assumption valid. Many scholars have already challenged its validity and disapproved it. In the words of Lt. Col. Vans Kennedy :

> "Are there any indications in history, tradition or affinity of language, which evince that a primeval tongue did actually exist 1200 years BC from which Greek and Sanskrit were derived? But it is evidently impossible to answer this question in the affirmative, or to produce any proofs of the prevalence of such a primeval tongue."

He goes further on to confirm the originality of Sanskrit as:

> "And the mere prevalence of such a primeval tongue; and the mere supposition, therefore that it may have existed is not sufficient to disapprove the perfect originality of Sanskrit."

He again questions the entity of primeval tongue :

> "If that tongue existed where, then, are the words of this primeval tongue to be found, and, if it be now extinct, how are the words supposed to belong to it and to be still preserved in Sanskrit to be ascertained,"

At last we can safely and unhesitatingly maintain that

supposition has no place in science and any inference made out of supposed statements can never be the science, but the travesty of science which would lead to the permanent closure of the subject under discussion. So if we want to open up further vistas of research in the filed of origin and development of languages, we shall have to drop the idea of existence of Proto-Indo-European language and shall have to concentrate around Sanskrit which is evidently and undisputedly is the source of all other languages.[1]

The present work is dedicated to the problem of origin and development languages in general and European languages in particular. Every Indian is well aware of the fact that all Indian vernaculars have sprung up from their mother, Sanskrit. English is only the foreign tongue which is widely spoken in India. So it would be interesting and pleasing to every Indian to know how this language was also born or evolved traditionally from Sanskrit. In this regard we get the first clue from Maharishi Dayananda's statement made by him during the course of his lectures in Pune. On Saturday, July 10,1875, he spoke thus :

> "Sanskrit is the root cause of all the languages. The languages like English found their origin or genesis traditionally in Sanskrit. One Language is degenerated from the other. English 'we' sprang up from Sanskrit *vayam* with the vocalization of *vayam.* Similarly from *pitara* (Sanskrit) came pater (Latin) and father (English); from *yuyam* came 'you' and from *ādim,* 'Adem', etc. This type of degeneration is sometimes bound with certain rules and sometimes takes place accidentally. No explanation is needed to scholars in this regard."[2]

---

[1] In this regard we may also refer to Dr. Gopal (1983 : Intro. 3). According to him, "Although a common Indo-European Origin for all cognate words found in Sanskrit, Greek and Latin is postulated by modern philologists and Sanskrit is not accepted as their primary source, it cannot be gainsaid that the oldest form of cognate words has been preserved in the Vedic language."

[2] ===संस्कृत सारी भाषाओं का मूल है। अंग्रेजी सदृश भाषाएं उससे परम्परा से उपन्न हुई। एक भाषा दूसरी भाषा का अपभ्रंश होकर उत्पन्न होती है। 'वयम' इस शब्द सं 'यम' को सम्प्रसारण होकर अंग्रेजी का 'वूई' (we) यह शब्द उत्पन्न हुआ। उसी प्रकार 'पितर' से 'पेतर' (लैटिन) और फादर (अंग्रेजी) 'यूयम' से 'यू' ;लवनद्ध और

Before I explain and elucidate this idea of traditional evolution of English, I would like to quote Mary Serjeantson who devoted his lot of precious time to search out foreign loan words in English. Though the author of present lines is not fully agree with his observations, still some of his findings and conclusions shed an ample good light on how English finds a traditional origin in Sanskrit by inheriting words from it through Greek and Latin? He observes, thus:

> "English has borrowed a few words, some directly and some indirectly, from Sanskrit, and these are among the very latest and very earliest from the East. Already in the old English period, and previously on the continent (as has been pointed out in chapter II), a few Sanskrit words had passed into Germanic or English through Greek and Latin."[1]

Here Mary Serjeantson makes a mention of a few Sanskrit words only, but I have discovered a long list of words which were inherited by English from its mother, Sanskrit either directly or through many other European Languages.

Here is the list of Sanskrit words which are borrowed traditionally by English via many other European languages.

(List showing traditional evolution of English-vocabulary from Sanskrit.

आदिम से आदम ;।कंउद्ध इत्यादि। ऐसे अपभ्रंश यथेच्छाचार से भी होते हैं। इसके बारे में बुद्धिमानों को कहने की कुछ आवश्यकता नहीं। =

See Bhartiya, V.S. 2042 : 28-29

1 *Op. cit.* 220-226.

	1	2	3	4	5
1. *Sanskrit*	*manu/mānava*	*pitṛ*	*mātṛ*	*bhrātṛ*	*svasṛ*
2. Latin	-	pater	-	frater	swesor
3. Greek	-	pater	- phrater		-
4. Old Slav.	-	-	- -	-	
5. Avesta	-	-	- -		-
6. Lithuanian	-	-	- -		-
7. Gothic	manna	-	-	swistar	
8. Old Norse	maer	-	mooir	-	systir
9. Old Saxon	man	-	modar		swestar
					swester
10. Old Frishian	man, mon	-	modar	-	suster, sister,
11. Old Irish	-	-	māthir	-	-
12. Velsh	-	-	- brawd	-	
13. Lettish	-	-	-	-	-
14. Middle Dutch	-	-	-	-	suster
15. Modern Dutch	man	-	moeder	-	zuster
16. Swedish	-	- -	-	-	
17. Old French	-	-	-	-	
18. Middle French	-	-	- -	-	
19. Modern French	-	-	- -		
20. Old German	man	-	muotar	-	swester
21. Middle German	-	-	- -	-	
22. German	mann	vater	mootter	bruder	schwester
23. Old English	man (n)	faeder	modor	brothor	sweoster
	man (n)			swister	
				swyster	
			suster		
24. Middle English	-	-	-	-	-
25. Modern English	Man	father	mother	brother	sister

	6	7	8	9	10	11
1.	*sunu,* (*suta*)	*duhitṛ*	*vāmā*	*vidhavā*	*purohita*	*puruṣa*
2.		-	-	-	praepositus	persōna 'mask'
3.		thugater	-	-	-	phersu
4.		-	-	-	-	-
5.		duyoar	-	vāduvā	-	-
6.		-	-	-	-	-
7.	sunus	dauhtar	-	widuwo	-	-
8.	sunr, sonr	dottir	-	-	-	-
9.	sunu, synu	dohtar	-	widowa	prçstar	-
10.	sunu	dochter	-	widwe	-	-
11.	suth (sutu)	-	-	-	-	-
12.		-	-	-	-	-
13.		-	-	-	-	-
14.		-	-	weduwe	-	-
15.	zoon	dochter	-	weduwe	-	-
16.	-	-	-	-	-	-
17.	-	-	-	vedue	prevost	persone, persoune
18.	-	-	-	-	-	-
19.	-	-	-	veuve	prevot	-
20.	sunu	tohter	-	wituwa witawa	prçstar	-
21.	-	-	-	witewe witwe	-	-
22.	sohn	tochter	-	witwe	-	-
23.	sunu	dohtor	wifman wife-man wimman	widewe widuwe wuduwe	prçost	- -
24.	-	-	wimman wumman	widewe widwe	prest	persone persoum
25.	son	daughter	woman	widow	priest	person

	12.	13.	14.	15.	16.	17.
1.	*sabhā* (*samāja*)	*ṛṣi*	*paritaṭṛ*	*spaœ*	*gallaḥ*	*donta*
2.	civilis 'pertaining to a citizen'	-	Protectus	specere 'To see'	-	dentem
3.	-	-	-	-	Glothis 'mouth of the wind pipe'	-
4.	-	-	-	-	-	-
5.	-	-	-	-	-	-
6.	šeim a, šeimyna	-	-	-	-	-
7.	haims 'village'	-	-	-	-	-
8.	-	-	-	spā 'to prophesy'	-	-
9.	semī ja 'family'	-	-	spāhi 'prudent'	-	-
10.	-	-	-	-	-	-
11.	-	-	-	-	-	-
12.	-	-	-	-	-	-
13.	sáime	-	-	-	-	-
14.	-	-	-	Spien 'to spy'	-	-
15.	-	-	-	-	-	-
16.	-	-	-	-	-	
17.	-	recercher	protectour	espier	-	-
18.	-	-	-	-	-	-
19.	civilis	-	-	espier	-	denen
20.	-	-	-	Spehōn	-	-
21.	-	-	-	sphen	-	-
22.	-	-	-	spähen	-	-
23.	-	-	-	-	-	-
24.	-	-	Protectour	spien espien	-	-
25.	civil	researcher	protector	Spy	glotin	dent

18	19	20	21	22	23
1. *udras*	*hanus, cibuka*	*nakhas*	*nāsā*	*pāda*	*bhrū*
2. -	gena	-	nāres	Ped	-
3. hudros 'water snake' hýdra'hydra'	gnathas	-	-	Pod	ophrus
4. -	-	-	-	-	-
5. -	-	-	-	-	-
6. udra	zandas	nagas	Nósis	pedu	-
7. -	kinnus	-	-	fotus	-
8. otr	kinni	nagal	Nasar	fótr	-
9. uydra	kinni	nagal	nose	fōt, fuot	-
10. -	kin	Neil	Nose	-	-
11. -	gin	-	-	-	-
12. -	-	-	-	-	-
13. -	-	-	-	-	-
14. -	-	-	nose, nuese	-	-
15. otter	kin	nagel	neus	voet	-
16. -	-	-	-	-	-
17. -	-	-	-	-	-
18. -	-	-	-	-	-
19. -	-	-	-	-	-
20. ottar	chinni	nayal	nasa	fuog	-
21. -	-	-	-	-	-
22. otter	kinn	nagel	nase	Fuss	-
23. otr, otar ottor	cin (n)	naegel, naegl	nosu	fōt	brú
24. -	-	-	-	-	-
25. otter	chin	Nail	nose	Foot	brow (eye)

24.	25.	26.	27.	28.	29.
1. *mukha*	*hasta*	*hṛt,hṛd*	*Plihan*	*mudrā*	*hikkā*
2. mentum	-	-	Sptçn	-	-
3. -	-	-	Splçn	-	-
4. -	-	-	-	-	-
5. -	-	-	Spçrçzan	-	-
6. -	-	-	-	-	-
7. -	handus	hairto	-	Mōps 'courage anger'	hixit
8. munpaz	Hond	hjarta	-	Mōor 'anger, wrath'	-
9. mūth, mund	Hand	herta	-	mōd,'mind, intellect heart'	-
10. mūth	-	herte	-	mōd,'mind intellect, heart	-
11. -	-	-	-	-	-
12. -	-	-	-	-	-
13. -	-	-	-	-	-
14. -	-	-	-	moet	-
15. mond	Hand	hart	-	moed	hik, hikken
16. -	-	-	-	-	-
17. -	-	-	Esplen	-	-
18. -	-	-	-	-	-
19. -	-	-	-	-	hoquet
20. mund	Hant	herza	-	muot	-
21. -	-	-	-	muot	-
22. -	hand	herza	-	mut 'courage'	-
23. mūp	hand	heorte	-	mōd,'mind' heart'	-
24. -	-	-	-	mode,mood	Hiccup
25. mouth	Hand	heart	Spleen	mood[1]	Hiccou

[1] According to Earnest Klein (475), the origin of these Teutonic words is uncertain, But here it is obvious that their origin can be traced to Sanskrit *mudrā.*

	30	31	32	33	34	35
1.	*mūḍha*	*koṣṭhab-addhatā*	*manas*	*kafa*	*svid* <*sveda*	*anya, apara*
2.	-	constīpātiō	mçns		-	-
3.	-	-	ménos	-	-	-
4.	-	-	-	-	-	-
5.	-	-	-	-	-	Anyas
6.	-	-	-	-	-	añtras 'from *anyatara- Skt.'*
7.	-	-	gamunds, muns	-	-	Annarr
8.	-	-	minni	-	-	Annarr
9.	gi-mçd	-	minnea	-	-	andaar
10.	-	-	mine	-	-	ōther
11.	-	-	-	-	-	-
12.	-	-	-	-	-	-
13.	-	-	-	-	-	-
14.	-	-	minne	cochen	-	-
15.	-	-	-	kuchen 'to cough'	-	Ander
16.	-	-	-	-	-	-
17.	-	-	-	-	-	-
18.	-	-	-	-	-	-
19.	-	-	-	-	-	-
20.	gir-meit 'foolish, crazy'	-	gimunt	-	-	Andar
21.	-	-	-	kūchen 'to breath'	-	-
22.	-	-	minne	kenchen	-	Ander
23.	gem āedd gemāeded, pp of gemad	-	gemynd 'memory'	cohhian	swat	ōper
24.	mad, madde	-	mind, mynd minde, munde	cowhen caughen	swet	-
25.	mad	Constipation	mind	Cough	sweat	

	36	37	38	39	40	41	42	43
1.	*tat*	*atra*	*anta*	*upari*	*Tatra*	*Pare, pūrva*	*nairṛti*	*īśāna*
2.	topper	-	-	supra 'from Skt. Sarvopari	-	prae 'before'	-	-
3.	to	-	-	-	Parai	-	"eneroi" 'those' below	?eos
4.	-	-	-	-	-	-	-	-
5.	-	-	-	-	-	-	-	-
6.	-	-	-	-	-	prç	-	-
7.	-	her	-	-	Thar	faura	-	-
8.	pat (that)	her	-	upp	Thar	-	noror	auster 'from the east'
9.	that	her, hir	-	-	-	pri	north	ōstar 'to east'
10.	thet	-	-	-	Ther	-	north	-
11.	-	-	-	-	-	-	-	-
12.	-	-	-	-	-	-	-	-
13.	-	-	-	-	-	-	-	-
14.	-	-	-	upper	-	-	nort, noort	-
15.	dat	hier	einde	op, opper	Daar	-	-	oost oosten
16.	-	-	-	-	-	-	-	-
17.	-	-	-	-	-	-	-	-
18.	-	-	-	-	-	-	-	-
19.	-	-	-	-	-	pre	-	-
20.	daz	hiar	-	uf	dār	-	nord	ōstar 'to east'
21.	-	-	-	-	-	-	nord	-
22.	das	hier	ende	auf	Da	-	nord	-
23.	Thaet	her	ende	up,upp uppan	thāer thçr	fore	noro	Çast 'in the east'
24.	-	-	-	uppon uppen	-	-	nora	East east
25.	that	here	end	up, upper	There	pre	north	East

	44	45	46	47	48	49	
1.	*vāyavaḥ*	*pārśva*	*sapta*	*eka*	*duan*	*trayas (masc.)* *tri* (fem.) *trīṇi* (neut.)	
2.	-	portiō	septem	unus	duo dual	trçs, tria	
3.	-	-	hepta	oios	dūo	treis, tria	
4.	-	-	-		-		
5.	-	-	-	açva	-	-	
6.	-	-	septyni	vienas	du	-	
7.	-	-	sibun	ains	twai (m.) twas (fem.) tuan (neut.)	threis,thrija	
8.	vestr		sjau	einn	their (m) tuaer (fem) tuan (neut)	thrir, thriar thriu	
9.	-	-	sibun	çn	twā, twō twé	-	
10.	west	-	sigun, seven	ān, én	twā	thrç, threa,	
11.	-		sechtn	-	-	-	
12.	- -		-	-	-	-	
13.	-		-	-	-	-	-
14.	west	-	-	-	-	-	
15.	west	-	zeven	een	twei	drie	
16.	-		-	-	-	-	-
17.	-	porcion	-	-	-	-	
18.	-		-	-	-	-	-
19.	ouest	portion	-	-	-	-	
20.	west 'only in compounds'	-	sibun	ein	zwā, zwō zwei (neut)	drī, drīo, driu	
21.	west	-	-	-	-	-	
22.	west	-	sieben	ein	zwei	drei	
23.	west (adv.) 'to the west'	-	seafon	ān	twā	thrī, thrie	
24.	west	-	-	an	-	-	
25.	west	portion	seven	one	two	three	

	50	51	52	53	54	55	56
1.	*pañcan*	*saṣ, saṭ*	*aṣṭau*	*navan*	*daśan*	*pañcadaśa*	*aṣṭādaśa*
2.	quinque	sex	octō	noven	decem	-	-
3.	pente, pempe	hex	oktō	ennéa deseti	dçka	-	-
4.	-	-	-	-	deseti		
5.	-	-	asta	-	-	-	-
6.	penki	-	astuoni	-	-	-	-
7.	fimf	saihs	ahtan		niun	taihun	fimftaihun
8.	fimm	sex	atta	niu	tiu	fimtan	attajan
9.	-	sehs	anto	-	tehan	fīfiein	ahtotian
10.	fif	sex	achta achte	nigun	tian tene fīne	fīftein	achatine
11.	-	sç	ocht	noi, noin	-	-	-
12.	-	-	-	-	-	-	-
13.	-	-	-	-	-	-	-
14.	-	-	-	-	-	-	-
15.	vijf	zes	acht	negen	tien	vijftien	achttien
16.	-	-	-	-	-	-	-
17.	-	-	-	-	-	-	-
18.	-	-	-	-	-	-	-
19.	-	-	-	-	-	-	-
20.	fimf, finf	schs	-	niun	zehan	fimfzehan	ahtozehan
21.	-	-	-	-	-	-	-
22.	fühf	sechs	acht	neun	zehn	fünfzehn	achtzehn
23.	fif	siex, syx, seox, seox, sex	ehta, eahta, ahta ahta	nigon	ten (e)	fiftçne	ehtatene, ahtatene
24.	-	-	-	-	-	-	-
25.	five	six	eight	nine	ten	fifteen	eighteen

	57	58	59	60	61	62	63
1.	*pañcāsat*	*ṣaṣṭiḥ*	*aśītiḥ*	*prathama*	*pratiśat*	*ad*	*kṛ*
2.	-	-	-	primus	percentum	edese	creare
3.	-	-	-	prétas	-	edein	-
4.	-	-	-	-	-	jami	-
5.	-	-	-	-	-	-	-
6.	-	-	-	-	-	edmi	-
7.	fimfigjus	-	-	-	-	itan	-
8.	fimmtigr	-	-	jyrstr	-	eta	-
9.	fiftich	-	-	furist	-	etan	-
10.	fiftich	-	achtich	-	-	eta	-
11.	-	-	-	-	-	ith	-
12.	-	-	-	-	-	-	-
13.	-	-	-	-	-	-	-
14.	-	-	-	-	-	-	-
15.	vijftig	-	-	-	-	eten, aat	
16.	-	-	-	-	-	-	-
17.	-	-	-	-	-	-	-
18.	-	-	-	-	-	-	-
19.	-	-	-	-	-	-	-
20.	fimfzug	-	-	furist	-	ezzan	-
21.	-	-	-	-	-	-	-
22.	fünfzig	sechszig	achtzig	fürst	-	essen	-
23.	fifig	sientig	hunde (a) htatig	fyrst, fyrest	-	eatan açt	-
24.	-	-	ezteti	-	-		creare
25.	fifty	sixty	eighty	first	percent	eat	create

	64	65	66	67	68	69	70
1.	*gam*	*chad*	*jan*	*bhū* *bhavati*	*santi*	*asti*	*asmi*
2.	-	-	-	-	sunt	est	esem, sum
3.	-	-	-	-	essi	esti	eimi
4.	-	-	-	byti	-	jesti	jesmi
5.	-	-	-	-	-	-	-
6.	-	-	-	buti	-	-	esmi
7.	geen	skdus	-	-	sind	ist	im
8.	-	-	-	-	-	es	em
9.	gān	scato	-	bium, biom	sind, sin	ist	em, bço 'akin to Skt. *bhavāmi*'
10.	gan, gçn	-	-	bim	send	is	-
11.	-	-	-	buith	it	is	am
12.	-	-	-	-	-	-	-
13.	-	-	-	-	-	-	-
14.	-	-	-	-	-	-	-
15.	gaan	schauw	-	ben	-	is	-
16.	-	-	-	-	-	-	-
17.	-	-	-	-	-	-	-
18.	-	-	-	-	-	-	-
19.	-	-	generate	-	-	-	-
20.	gān,scato 'present', gām	-	bim	sint	ist	-	
21.	-	-	-	-	-	-	-
22.	gehen	schatte	-	-	-	ist	bin
23.	gān, gā	sceadu	-	-	sind,	is	eam, am
24.	-	-	-	-	sindon	-	-
25.	go	shadow	generate	be	are	is	am

	71	72	73	74	75
1.	*milati*	*luk, lokati*	*carvana*	*dānam*	*vi+naśa*
2.	-	-	-	dōnā tiōnnem	evānescere
3.	-	-	-	doron	-
4.	-	-	-	dani 'tribute'	-
5.	-	-	-	-	-
6.	-	-	-	duonis 'gift'	-
7.	-	-	-	-	-
8.	mōeta	-	-	-	-
9.	mōtian	lōkon	-	dar 'gift'	-
10.	mçta	lōkia	-	-	-
11.	-	-	-	-	-
12.	-	-	-	-	-
13.	-	-	-	-	-
14.	-	locken	-	-	-
15.	moeten	-	kauwen[1]	-	-
16.	-	-	-	-	-
17.	-	-	-	-	`e(s) vanir
18.	-	-	-	-	-
19.	-	-	-	dīnātiōnnem	-
20.	-	luogçn	kiuwan[1]	-	-
21.	-	-	kiuwen[1]	-	-
22.	sammeln cp. Skt. *sammelana*	lugen	kauen[1]	-	-
23.	mçtan	lōcian	ceōwan	-	-
24.	-	-	chewen	-	-
25.	meat	look	chew	donation	vanish

[1] The change of *c* into *k* owes to Pāṇ. rule *coḥ kuḥ* 8.2.30

	76	77	78	79	80
1.	*smera, smayati*	*seva*	*heḍa*	*kruśa* *krośati*	*vam >* *vamati*
2.	-	servire	-	crucem	vomitus
3.	-	-	-	-	khmein 'to vomit'
4.	smijati, smejo	-	-	-	-
5.	-	-	-	-	vam'spit'
6.	-	-	-	-	vemtú, vémti 'to vomit'
7.	-	-	hatan	-	-
8.	-	-	hata, hatr	kross	1.vāeme 'sea sickness' 2. vāma 'nausea'
9.	-	-	haton	kruzi	-
10.	-	-	hatia	-	-
11.	-	-	-	cros	-
12.	-	-	-	-	-
13.	-	-	-	-	-
14.	-	-	-	crūce	-
15.	-	-	haten	-	-
16.	-	-	-	-	-
17.	-	servir	-	-	-
18.	-	-	-	-	vomite, vomit
19.	-	-	croix		-
20.	smierōn	-	hazzon	krūzi	-
21.	-	-	-	kriuze	-
22.	schmieren	-	hassen	kreuz	-
23.	smerian, smearcian	-	hatian	cros	
24.	-	-		cros	vomet,vomit
25.	smile	serve	hate	cross	vomit

81	82	83	84	85
1. *vi, vāchi* *vása* *van<vanati*	*sad<sīdati*	*sī, swap*	*sam+gī*	*pra+car*
2. vemus 'love'	-	-	-	praedicāre 'to cry in public'
3. -	kszeathai 'to sit'	-	'omth'n 'voice oracle'	- -
4. -	sittian	slāpan	singan	-
5. -	-	-	-	-
6. -	-	-	-	-
7. -	sitan	-	siggwan	-
8. āeskja	sitja	-	-	-
9. - -	-	-		-
10. -	sitta	slçpa	sianga, siunga	-
11. -	-	-	-	-
12. -	-	-	-	-
13. -	-	-	-	-
14. wonscen wūnscen wenscen	sitten	slapen	singher	-
15. wensen	zitten	slapen	zingen	-
16. o?nska	sitta	-	sjunga	-
17. -	-	-	-	preechier
18. -	-	-	-	-
19. -	-	-	-	-
20. wunsken	sizzan	slafan	singen	-
21. wansch	sitzen	slafen	singen	-
22. wansch	sitzen	slafen	singen	-
23. wȳscan	sittan	slāepan	singan	-
24. wisshen	sitten	sleper	singen	precher
25. wish	sit	sleep	sing	preach

	86	87	88	89	90	91
1.	*āp, āpnoti*	*vana + vas*	*ambara*	*stṛ*	*valabhī*	*vāta, vāyu*
2.	obtenīre	-	ambare ambrum	-	-	ventus
3.	-	-	-	-	-	-
4.	-	-	-	-	-	vejati
5.	-	-	-	-	-	-
6.	-	-	-	-	-	vejas
7.	-	-	-	stairnō	-	winds
8.	-	-	-	stajarna	-	vindr
9.	-	-	-	sterro	-	wind
10.	-	-	-	stera	-	wind
11.	-	-	-	-	-	feth
12.	-	-	-	-	-	-
13.	-	-	-	-	-	-
14.	-	-	-	stjerna	-	-
15.	-	-	-	ster	-	wind
16.	-	-	-	sttjerna	-	-
17.	-	baniss	ambre	-	-	-
18.	ōbtenir	-	-	-	-	-
19.	obtenir	bannir 'to banish'	-	-	-	-
20.	-	-	-	sterro	balcho 'beam'	wint
21.	-	-	-	sterre	balke	-
22.	-	-	Ambra	-	-	wind
23.	-	-	-	steorra	-	-
24.	obteinen	banishen	aumber	sterre	-	wind
25.	obtain	banishment	amber	star	balcony	wind

	92	93	94	95	96	97
1.	*vāri*	*rásmi*	*ghāsa*	*candana*	*jaṅgala*	*karpūra*
2.	-	-	-	-	-	camphora
3.	-	-	-	-	-	kaphourd
4.	-	-	-	-	-	-
5.	-	-	-	-	-	-
6.	-	-	-	-	-	-
7.	wato	-	gras	-	-	-
8.	vatn	-	gras	-	-	-
9.	watar-	gras	-	-	-	
10.	weter	-	gres,gers-		-	-
11.	-	-	-	-	-	-
12.	-	-	-	-	-	-
13.	-	-	-	-	-	-
14.	-	-	-	-	-	-
15.	water	-	gras	-	-	-
16.	-	-	-	-	-	-
17.	-	rai	-	sandal	-	camphore
18.	-	-	-	sandre, sandale, santal	-	comphre
19.	-	rai, rais 'spoke of what'	-	-	jungle	-
20.	wazzar	-	gras	-	-	-
21.	-	-	-	-	-	-
22.	wasser	-	gras	sandanon, santalon	dschungel-	
23.	waeter	rai,	graes, gaess	- -	-	-
24.	-	-	-	sandalum	-	-
25.	water	ray	grass	sandal	jungle	camphor

	98	99	100	101	102	103	104
1.	*horā*	*muhūrta*	*skandha*	*syona*	*divā*	*nakta*	*śati*
2.	hōra 'hour'	minūta	secunda	-	dies	noct,nox	centuria
3.	orā 'any time'	-	-	-	-	nux, nukt	-
4.	-	-	sunna	-	-	nosti	-
5.	-	-	-	-	-	-	-
6.	-	-	-	-	-	-	-
7.	-	-	sunno	-	-	nahts	-
8.	-	-	sunna	-	-	nátt, nótt	-
9.	-	-	-	-	-	naht	-
10.	-	-	sunne	-		nacht	-
11.	-	-	-	-	-	-	-
12.	-	-	-	-	-	-	-
13.	-	-	-	-	-	-	-
14.	-	-	-	-	-	nacht	-
15.	-	-	zon	-	day	nacht	-
16.	-	-	-	-	-	-	-
17.	ure, ore hore	-	-	-	-	-	-
18.	-	-	-	-	-	-	-
19.	heure	minute	seconde	-	-	-	-
20	-	-	sunna	-		naht	-
21.	-	-	sonne	-	tag	nacht	-
22.	-	-	sunne	-	daey	niht	-
23.	hour	minute	-	-		-	-
24	-	-	-	-	-	-	-
25.	hour	minute	second	sun	day	night	century

	105	106	107	108	109	110
1.	*sāmivatsara*	*hyas*	*madhyāhna*	*kuṭī*	*dvāra, dura*[1]	*aṭṭaḥ*
2.	sçmestris	-	meridiānus	-	fores	-
3.	semestris	-	-	-	thúrā	-
4.	-	-	-	-	dvirī	-
5.	-	-	-	-	dvarém (acc. sg.)	-
6.	-	-	-	-	dúrys	-
7.	-	-	-	-	dour	-
8.	-	-	-	kot	dyrr	-
9.	-	-	-	-	duru	-
10.	-	-	-	-	dur, dore	-
11.	-	-	-	-	-	-
12.	-	-	-	-	-	-
13.	-	-	-	-	-	-
14.	-	-	-	cot,cote	-	-
15.	-	-	-	kot	-	-
16.	-	-	-	-	-	-
17.	-	geostram	meridian	-	-	-
18.	-	-	-	-	-	-
19.	-	-	meridien	-	-	attique
20.	-	-	-	-	turi	-
21.	-	-	-	-	tür	-
22.	-	-	-	-	tur	-
23.	-	-	-	cot	dor, duru	-
24.	-	-	-	cot, cote	dore, ture	-
25.	semester	yester	meridian	cot, cottage	door	attic

[1] Cf. *śatadura* 'hundred doors' *RV.* 1.51.3.

	111	112	113	114 115	116	
1.	*aspatāla*	*maśka*	*mūṣa (ka)*	*sarpa*	*hari*	*catuṣpada*
2.	hospitale	musca 'fly'	mūs	serpçns	ros, ors	-
3.	-	-	mūs	ksrpein	-	-
4.	-	-	myši	-	-	-
5.	-	-	-	-	-	-
6.	-	-	-	-	-	-
7.	-	-	-	-	-	-
8.	-	-	mūs	-	hross	-
9.	-	-	mūs	-	hros	-
10.	-	-	mūs	-	hors, hars	-
11.	-	-	-	-	-	-
12.	-	-	-	-	-	-
13.	-	-	-	-	-	-
14.	-	-	-	-	ors	-
15.	-	-	muis	-	ros	-
16.	-	-	-	-	-	-
17.	-	-	-	serpent	-	-
18.	-	-	-	-	-	-
19.	-	-	-	serpent	-	-
20.	hospital	-	mūs	-	hros, ros	-
21.	-	-	-	-	-	-
22.	-	-	maus	-	roβ (jumping animal)	-
23.	-	-	mus	-	hors	-
24.	-	-	-	serpent	hors	-
25.	hospital	mosquito	mouse	serpant	horse	quadruped

	117	118	119	120	121	122	123	
1.	*faṇa*	*piṭhara*	*rajjū*	*patra*	*vastrī*	*kapāla*	*swiṣṭa*	
2.	vangen	pottus	-	papȳrus	vastiārium	cappe	-	
3.	-	-	-	papūras	-		edus	
4.	-	-	-	-	-	-	-	
5.	-	-	-	-	-	-	-	
6.	-	-	-	-	-	-	-	
7.	fāhan-	raip	-	-	-	-		
			'shoe lace'					
8.	fanga, fā	-	reip	-		-	saétr	
9.	fāhan-	-	-		-	swōti		
10.	fangia	-	-	-	-	-	-	
11.	-	-	-	-	-	-	-	
12.	-	-	-	-	-	-	-	
13.	-	-	-	-	-	-	-	
14.	vangen	pot	reep	-	-	-	-	
15.	vangen	pot	reep	-	-	-	-	
16.	-	-	-	-	-	-	-	
17.	-	-	-	papier	-	-	-	
18.	-	-	-	-	vesliairie-		-	
					vastiaire			
19.	-	pot	-	-		-	-	-
20.	fāhan	-	reif	-	-		swuozi	
			'ring hoop'			chuph	suozi	
21.	vāhen	-	reif	papir	-	kopf	sūege	
22.	fangen	-	reif	papir	-	kopf	siüβ	
23.	fōn	pott	rāp	-	-	cuppe	swéte	
24.	fangen	pott	rop, rope	vestrye	cuppe	swete, swote		
25.	fangpot	rope	paper	vestry	cup	sweet		

	124	125	126	127	128
1.	*vastra*	*vāhana*	*manyā* *'collar'*	*miti*	*mātrika*
2.	vestitūra	-		metrum	metricus
3.	-	-		metron	metrist
4.	-	-		-	-
5.	-	-		-	-
6.	-	-		-	-
7.	-	-		-	-
8.	-	-	mon	-	-
9.	-	-	-	-	-
10.	-	-	mana	-	-
11.	-	-	-	-	-
12.	-	-	-	-	-
13.	-	-	-	-	-
14.	-	-	mane	-	-
15.	-	-	-	-	-
16.	-	-	-	-	-
17.	-	-	-	metre	-
18.	vesteure, vesture	wagen	-	-	-
19.	vesture	-	-	-	metrique
20.	-	-	-	-	-
21.	-	-	-	meter	-
22.	-	-	mähna	-	metrix
23.	-	-	manu	-	-
24.	vesteure vesture	-	-	-	-
25.	vesture	wagen	mane	metre	metric

129	130	131	132	133
1. *guru*	*gola*	*kṣudra*	*ulūka*	*kramela*
2. gravis	globus	-	ulula	camçlus
3. baros	-	-	-	khámçlos
4. -	-	-	-	
5. gouru	-	-	-	
6. -	-	-	-	
7. kaurus	-	-	-	
8. -	-	-	ugla	
9. -	-	-	-	
10. -	-	-	-	
11. -	-	-	-	
12. -	-	-	-	
13. -	-	-	-	
14. -	-	-	ūle	
15. -	-	-	uil	
16. -	-	-	-	
17. -	-	-	-	chamel
18. -	-	-	-	-
19. -	globus	-	-	chamean
20. -	-	scury	ūwile	-
21. -	-	-	iule	
22. -	-	-	eule	
23. -	-	sceort	ūle	camel
24. -	-	-	-	chamail, cameil camel, chamel
25. grave	glob	short	owl	camel

	134	135	136	137	138	139
1.	*kokila*	*akṣa*	*kaksa*	*pavitra*	*romāñca*	*sastra*
2.	cuculis scientia	arcia	classis	puru	-	
3.	kokkux	aninç	-	-	-	-
4.	-		-	-		-
5.	-		-	-	-	-
6.	-		-	-	-	-
7.	-		-	-	-	-
8.	-		-	-	-	-
9.	-		-	-	-	-
10.	-		-	-	-	-
11.	-		-	-	-	-
12.	-		-	-	-	-
13.	-		-	-	-	-
14.	-		-	-	-	-
15.	-		-	-	-	-
16.	-		-	-	-	-
17.	cucu	-	-	pur	romanz, romans	science
18.	-		-	-	-	-
19.	coucou	-	classe	-	romance	-
20.	-	acchus	-	-	-	-
21.	-	-	-	-	-	-
22.	-	ax, axt	-	-	-	-
23.	-	aex	-	-	-	-
24.	-		-	-	romanz, romaunz	-
25.	cuckoo	axe	class	pure	romance	science

	140	141	142	143	144	145
1.	*sabda, svana*	*nava*	*nāman*	*vāta*	*aphenaṁ*	*ṛchate*
2.	sonus	-	nōmen	ventus	opium	rigit
3.	-	-	-	-	opion	(o) regetai
4.	-	novū	-	vejati	-	-
5.	-	nava	-	-	-	-
6.	-	-	-	vajar	-	-
7.	svanr	nivijis	-	winds	-	-
8.	-	nȳr	-	vindr	-	-
9.	-	nivi, nivuri	-	wind	-	-
10.	-	nīe	-	wind	-	-
11.	-	-	-	-	-	-
12.	-	-	-	-	-	-
13.	-	-	-	-	-	-
14.	-	nūwe, nie nieuwe		-	-	- -
15.	-	nievw	-	wind	-	-
16.	-	-	-	-	-	-
17.	son	-	non, nom	-	-	-
18.	-	-	-	-	-	-
19.	son	-	nom	-	-	-
20.	-	nivwi	-	wint	-	-
21.	-	nivwé	-	-	-	-
22.	geswin	neu nīwe	-	wind	opium	recket
23.	-	nçowe	-	wind	-	reacheth
24.	soun	newe new	nowne	-	-	-
25.	sound	new	noun	wind	opium	reach

	146	147	148	149	150	151
1.	*kalamam*	*jānu*	*tārā, stṛ*	*kalaśam*	*kupām*	*gala*
2.	calamum		sidera,	calathum,		
		genu	astrum	calycem	cupam	gula
3.	khalamon	gonu	teirea,astçr	khvlikha	-	-
				khalathov		
4.	-	-	-	-	-	-
5.	-	-	-	-	-	-
6.	-	-	-	-	-	-
7.	-	-	-	-	-	-
8.	-	-	-	-	-	-
9.	-	-	-	-	-	-
10.	-	-	-	-	-	-
11.	-	-	-	-	-	-
12.	-	-	-	-	-	-
13.	-	-	-	-	-	-
14.	-	-	-	-	-	-
15.	-	-	-	-	-	-
16.	-	-	-	-	-	
17.	-	-	-	-	-	-
18.	-	-	-	-	-	-
19.	-	-	-	-	-	-
20.	-	-	-	-	-	-
21.	-	-	-	-	-	-
22.	kiel	knie	stern	kelch	kufe	kehle
23.	-	-	-	-	-	-
24.	-	-	-	-	-	-
25.	quill	knee	star	chalice	coop	gullet

	152	153	154	155	156	157
1.	*grasate*	*gharmmam*	*corayati*	*cuṣayati*	*sthagate*	*tanum*
2.	-	thermon	urit	sugit	tegit	tenuem
3.	grasetai	-	-	-	stegetai	-
4.	-	-	-	-	-	-
5.	-	-	-	-	-	-
6.	-	-	-	-	-	-
7.	-	-	-	-	-	-
8.	-	-	-	-	-	-
9.	-	-	-	-	-	-
10.	-	-	-	-	-	-
11.	-	-	-	-	-	-
12.	-	-	-	-	-	-
13.	-	-	-	-	-	-
14.	-	-	-	-	-	-
15.	-	-	-	-	-	-
16.	-	-	-	-	-	-
17.	-	-	-	-	-	
18.	-	-	-	-	-	-
19.	-	-	-	-	-	-
20.	-	-	-	-	-	-
21.	-	-	-	-	-	-
22.	-	-	-	sauget	decket	dünne
23.	-	-	-	-	-	
24.	grazeth (A.S.)	-	churreth (A.S.)	sucketh (A.S.)	Theciath (A.S.)	-
25.	graze	thermal	-	suck	-	thin

	158	159	160	161	162	163
1.	*dame*[1]	*pārāvata*	*na,no, naiva*	*dāru druma, taru*	*pāthaḥ*[2]	*ṛta*
2.	-	-	ne	-	-	rçctus
3.	-	-	-	drūs	-	-
4.	-	-	ne	-	-	-
5.	-	-	ne	dāuru	-	-
6.	-	-	ne	-	-	
7.	-	-	ne	triu	-	raihtsr
8.	-	-	no	trç	bad	rçttr
9.	-	-	ne	trio, tree	bath	reht
10.	-	-	ne	trç	-	-
11.	-	-	-	-	-	-
12.	-	-	-	-	-	-
13.	-	-	-	-	-	-
14.	-	-	-	-	bat	-
15.	dame	-	-	-	bad	-
16.	dam	-	-	-	-	-
17.	-	-	-	-	-	-
18.	-	-	-	-	-	-
19.	-	parapetto	-	-	-	-
20.	-	-	ne	-	bad	reht
21.	-	-	-	-	bat	reht
22.	dame	-	-	-	bad	recht
23.	-	-	nā, nō	trçow	baed	riht
24.	-	-	na, no	tre, tree	bath	right,riht
25.	dame	parapet	no not	tree	bath	right

[1] *Dame has been enumerated in gṛhanāma (Nir. 3.4) gṛham* doesn't mean 'house' only, but it is also to mean 'house wife'. In this regard, we may note a popular maxim '*na gṛham gṛhamityāhur gṛhiṇi gṛhamucyate.*'

[2] In the *RV.* 1.47.33, Sāyaṇa translates *pāthas* as 'taken bath.' Actually the same Vedic *pātha* led to the origin of 'bath', etc. in the other European languages.

The above cited examples will suffice to understand the traditional evolution of English from Sanskrit.

Now, I would like to cut short and furnish an another list of words borrowed by English from Sanskrit either via Greek, Latin and German or via German only or sometimes directly from Sanskrit. This list also includes those old English terms which failed to survive by the time of modern English and sometimes Anglo-Saxon words have also been incorporated and as such they have beeb marked with A.S. so as to separate them from the rests, *i.e.* from Modern and Old English words.

	Sanskrit	**Greek**	**Latin**	**German**	**English**
164.	*tarman*	-	terminus	termin	term
165.	*tānam*	tonom	tonum	ton	tone
166.	*naddham*	-	nodum	knoton	knot
167.	*paru*	pur	-	feuer	fire
168.	*pardate*	bdeetai	pedit	-	farteth (fart)
169.	*puras*	paros	prae	vor	fore
170.	*prānta*	-	frontem	fronte	front
171.	*fullam*	phullon	folium	-	flower
172.	*phavate*	phvetai	fuit	-	beeth, beoth (A.S.)
173.	*bhrū*	ophrus	-	bravne	brow
174.	*madhu*	methu	-	meth	mead
175.	*manate*	mnaetai	monet	meynet	meaneth
176.	*mahatva*	megethos	-	macht	might
177.	*me*	me	me	-	me
178.	*mitam*	-	metitum	-	meted
179.	*mṛtam*	-	mortuum	-	mortal
180.	*yat*	-	id	-	it
181	*yuvan*	-	juvenis	jung	young

Sanskrit	Greek	Latin	German	English
182. *roṣa*	orgç	-	rasen	rage
183. *rohita*	ereuthon	-	roth	red
184 *lapana*	-	labium	lippe	lip
185. *locayati*	-	lucet	-	lixeth (A.S.)
186 *vakṣate*	aezetai	auget	wachset	waxeth
187. *varāhaḥ*	-	verses	-	boar,bare (A.S.)
188. *vastyayati*	-	vastat	wüstet	wasteth
189. *vepate*	uphaetai	-	webet	weaveth
190. *śāla*	skholç	schola	schule	school
191. *śṛnga*	-	cornu	horn	horn
192. *santaḥ*	-	sanctus	-	saint
193. *siwati*	-	suit	-	seweth
194. *sīdati*	-	cedet	-	cedeth
195. *svanitam*	-	sonitum	-	sound
196. *hanum*	genuu	-	kinn	chin
197. *ásanam*	-	-	essung	food
198. *nābhi*	-	-	nabe	nave
199. *bandhayati*	-	-	bindet	bind
200. *bukka*	-	-	bocke	he-goat
201. *śubha*	-	-	hübsch	handsome
202. *akṣi*	-	-	auge	eye
203. *āyasam*	-	-	eisen	iron
204. *ukṣā*	-	-	ochse	ox
205. *ubhayata*	-	-	beide	both
206. *kusyati*	-	-	küsset	kiss
207. *gati*	-	-	gehet	go
208. *ghāsa*	-	-	gras	grass
209. *calli*	-	-	schale	shell

	Sanskrit	Greek	Latin	German	English
210.	*cicheda*	-	-	schiede	divided
211.	*cinatti*	-	-	schneidet	cuts
212.	*tṛṣyati*	-	-	durstet	thirsty
213.	*dalati*	-	-	theilet	deal, daelath (A.S.)
214.	*divyati*	-	-	taget	daegiah(A.S.)
215.	*drākhitam*	-	-	trocken	dry
216.	*dhvanati*	-	-	donnet	dinneth
217.	*dhvani*	-	-	don	din
218	*palati*	-	-	fliehet	fleeth
219.	*fullati*	-	-	blühet	bloweth
220.	*pota*	-	-	boot	boat
221.	*fullati*	-	-	blühet	bloweth
222.	*badati*	-	-	badet	batheth
223.	*bhadra*	-	-	bieder	better
224.	*bhajati*	-	-	beuget	boweth
225.	*manuṣya*	-	-	menschheit	mankind
226.	*marcati*	-	-	marschirt	marcheth
227.	*marddhati*	-	-	marschirt	marcheth
228.	*muda*	-	-	muth	mood
229.	*laṣati*	-	-	lüstert	lusteth
230.	*vardaram*	-	-	wasser	water
231.	*vāsa*	-	-	haus	house
232.	*vāhanam*	-	-	wagen	wain, wagen
233.	*wega*	-	-	wege	way
234.	*veṇāti*	-	-	wahnet	weeneth
235.	*vela*	-	-	weile	while
236.	*stambha*	-	-	stumpf	stupid

	Sanskrit	Greek	Latin	German	English
237.	*sthalam*	-	-	stelle	stall
238.	*sthira*	-	-	stier	steer
239.	*syona*	-	-	sonne	sun
240.	*hansa*	-	-	gans	goose
241.	*ajra 'plain'*	ager	agros '*field*'	-	acre, agriculture
242.	*trikoṇamiti*	trigonov	trignometria	-	trignometry
243.	*takṣaka*	töeikhov	toxicum	-	tonic
244	*ātma, aṇu*	atomas	atomus	-	atom
245.	*amṛta*	immortal	-	immortle	
246.	*aveśa*	-	-	-	awise (A.S)
247.	*āvali*	-	-	-	alley
248.	*kuyati*	-	-	-	cooeth
249.	*kurula*	-	-	-	curl
250.	*komala*	-	-	-	comely
251.	*kwelati*	-	-	-	quaileth
252.	*kṣurati*	-	-	-	scoureth
253.	*khalati*	-	-	-	culleth
254.	*khārī*	-	-	-	scar
255.	*khyāti*	-	-	-	quoth
256.	*gaṇa*	-	-	-	ganoth (A.S.)
257.	*gati*	-	-	-	gait
258.	*garddha*	-	-	-	greed
259.	*ghraṣṭa*	-	-	-	grist
260.	*cāṭa*	-	-	-	cheat
261.	*cūrṇāyati*	-	-	-	churneth
262.	*chalayati*	-	-	-	sylath (A.S.)
263.	*juṣati*	-	-	-	re-joiceth
264.	*jhaṁpati*	-	-	-	jumpeth

	Sanskrit	Greek	Latin	German	English
265.	*tat*	-	-	-	that
266.	*tasati*	-	-	-	thosseth
267.	*tustam*	-	-	-	dust
268.	*torati*	-	-	-	teareth, tear
269.	*diyati*	-	-	-	dieth
270.	*māla*	-	-	-	male
271.	*mṛd*	-	-	-	mud
272.	*methati*	-	-	-	mateth
273.	*yāta*	-	-	-	yode
274.	*yuddha*	-	-	-	guthe (A.S.)
275.	*yuyam*	-	-	-	you
276.	*raṇati*	-	-	-	runneth
277.	*rudhira*	-	-	-	rodra, icelan
278.	*rodaḥ*	-	-		rodera (A.S.)
279.	*lavan*	-	-	-	leven
280.	*aham*	-	-	-	I
281.	*mama*	-	-	-	my
282.	*mām, me*	-	-	-	me
283.	*asmān*	-	-	-	us
284.	*tvam*	-	-	-	thou, you
285.	*tava*	-	-	-	thine, your
286.	*yasmān*	-	-	-	you
287.	*asau, saḥ*	-	-	-	he
288.	*amūm*	-	-	-	him
289.	*sā*	-	-	-	she
290.	*te*	-	-	-	they
291.	*tan*	-	-	-	them
292.	*idam*	-	-	-	it

Sanskrit	Greek	Latin	German	English
293. *asya*	-	-	-	its
294. *svaṣādaḥ*	-	-	-	suicide
295. *purogam*	-	-	-	programme
296. *cāru*	-	-	-	charming
297. *itaraḥ*	-	-	-	other
298. *durbalatā*	-	-	-	debility
299. *vṛndaḥ*	-	-	-	band
300. *supara*	-	-	-	supreme
301. *sūpam*	-	-	-	soup
302. *sīva*<*siva*	-	-	-	sew
303. *samitiḥ*	-	-	-	committee
304. *drapsaḥ*	-	-	-	drops
305. *khaṭvā*	-	-	-	cot
306. *piṅga*	-	-	-	pink[1]
307. *prokṣa*	-	-	-	proxy
308. *ukṣāṇa* (pl. of *ukṣā*)		-	-	6x
309. *nakta*	-	-	-	night
310. *gṛbha*	-	-	-	gripp, grab
311. *baliṣṭha*	-	-	-	bold
312. *nava*	-	-	-	novel
313. *balvāna*	-	-	-	valiant
314. *nava*	-	-	-	new
315. *naval*	-	-	-	novel
316. *naviṣṭha*	-	-	-	newest
317. *preṣṭha*	-	-	-	priest

[1] According to Dr. Earnest Klein (563), it is of uncertain origin. But its origin can easily be raced to Sanskrit *piṅga*.

	Sanskrit	Greek	Latin	German	English
318.	*udgama*	-	-	-	outcome
319.	*aho*	-	-	-	oh
320.	*ullāsa*	-	-	-	hurrah
321.	*āvarta*	-	-	-	avert
322.	*dipsati*	-	-	-	deception
323.	*tṛdla*	-	-	-	tread
324.	*ava*	-	-	-	obey
325.	*vadhu*	-	-	-	bride
326.	*śraddhālu*	-	-	-	credulous
327.	*śrddhit*	-	-	-	credit
328.	*daman*	-	-	-	dominate
329.	*bhiṣak*	-	-	-	physician
330.	*anusvara*	-	-	-	answer
331.	*svadate*	-	-	-	sweat
332.	*bandhan*	-	-	-	bond, bundle
333.	*avāsa*	-	-	-	abyss
334.	*svanika*	-	-	-	sonic
335.	*vāca*	-	-	-	voice
336.	*vācāla*	-	-	-	vocal
337.	*antara*	-	-	-	inter
338.	*mādhyam*	-	-	-	medium
339.	*pavitratā*	-	-	-	purity
340.	*puṇḍa*	-	-	-	pound
341.	*lubha*	-	-	-	love
342.	*lubhāvali*	-	-	-	lovely
343.	*vistar*	-	-	-	vast
344.	*sīva*	-	-	-	sew
345.	*sīvati*	-	-	-	seweth

	Sanskrit	Greek	Latin	German	English
346.	*snāyu*	-	-	-	sinew
347.	*eka*	-	-	-	equal
348.	*dama*	dome	-	-	home
349.	*krūta*	-	-	-	cruel
350.	*graddha*	-	-	-	greed
351.	*vid*	-	-	-	wit
352.	*jvala*	-	-	-	glow
353.	*tapa*	-	-	-	tepid
354.	*tṛṣita*	-	-	-	thirsty
355.	*trasa*	-	-	-	harras,terror
356.	*hṛd*	-	-	-	heart
357.	*agni*	-	-	-	ignis, ignite
358.	*rakta*	-	-	-	red
359.	*chav*	-	-	-	chew
360.	*plāyate*	-	-	-	fly
361.	*nāma*	-	-	-	name
362.	*pāda*	-	-	-	foot
363.	*krimi*	-	-	-	germ
364.	*ṛju*	-	-	-	right
365.	*dakṣiṇa*	-	-	-	deccan

Thus hosts of similar other examples may be cited, but the author doesn't think it necessary to produce all of them here.

Evolution of the English-grammatical structure

Besides borrowing a large number of its vocabulary, English owes a lot to Sanskrit for evolving its usage, diction and style. A few illustrations in this regard may be made as under.

1. *Elision of sounds* : In Sanskrit, elision of one or two sounds is a common feature. In this regard *Bṛhaddevatā* of Śaunaka (2.116) maintains thus, *varṇasya varṇayor lopo bahunām vyañjanasya ca. atrāṇī kapirnābhā dano yāmityaghāus ca.*

English has also developed similar tendency of elision of one or more sounds as :

do not →	don't	
cannot	→	can't
will not	→	won't
shall not	→	shan't

2. *Syntactical placement of 'no'* : English negative particle 'no' had evolved from Sanskrit *na* or *no.* In Sanskrit, especially the Vedic Sanskrit, it anteceeds the word it negates, *e.g.*

Nendram devam-amansata (*RV.* 10.86.1) Yāska has made similar observations in this regard. According to him, *purastādupacārs tasya yat pratiṣedhati i.e. na* is placed before the word it negates.

This trend of the Vedic language was traditionally accepted in the English. It places 'no' before the negated word, *e.g.* 'I have no book', here 'no' precedes the book. On the other hand, in Classical Sanskrit or Hindi, we don't meet with any strict rule regarding the syntactical employment of 'no'. In these languages, it may precede or succeed the word it negates.

3. *Infinitives* : Sometimes English seem to adopt Sanskrit forms and rules more perfectly and regularly even than Hindi. For instance, Sanskrit infinitive suffix - *tumun* or - *tum* is accepted in English as 'to'. Sanskrit *saḥ gantum (gam+tum) icchati* will be read in English as 'He wants to go'; *saḥ paṭhitum (gam+tum)* will be read as 'He wants to read'. Here, the only difference is that Sanskrit '*-tum*' has changed its position in English from suffix or post-position to pre-position.

4. *Compounds* : In Sanskrit Negative Determinative Compound (*Nañ Tatpuruṣa*) enjoins '*a*' before a noun beginning with a vowel (*e.g. an + aśva*). English has also inherited this tendency from Sanskrit with a slight variation. It drops '*a*' altogether and invariably uses *an* as 'un' without any discrimination of vowel or consonant, *e.g.* un-known, un-able, un-do, etc. The other difference is that in Sanskrit *a* or *an* are employed with nominal forms, whereas in English 'un' is employed only with verbal forms.

5. *Euphonic combinations* : In Sanskrit, any consonant followed by a nasal sound will be substituted by a nasal or a word pronounced as nasal. Cf. Pāṇ. (8.4.45) *yaro'nunāsike' nunāsiko vā.* And *vārt.* (on Pāṇ. 8.4.45) *pratyaye bhāṣāyāṁ nityam.*

Examples are : *tad +mātram = tanmātram*

cit + mayam = cinmayam

etad + murārī = etanmurārī

English has borrowed similar type of tendency. In it, consonants, when come in proximity with an un-interrupted nasal sound, become silent and pronounced as a nasal itself, *e.g.* mnemonic, mnematics, gnarl, gnash, gnat, gnaw, gnome, gnomon, Gnostic, gnu, knack, knag, knap, knar, knave, knead, knee, knell, knife, knit, knob, know, pneumatic, pneumonia, pneumatics, etc.

6. *Laws of doubling* : English doubles its consonants under the following situations.

(i) Words of one syllable having one vowel and ending in a single consonant double the consonant before a suffix beginning with a vowel, such as runner, hitting, knitted.

(ii) Two or three syllable words ending in a single consonant following a single vowel double the final consonant when the stress falls on the last syllable, *e.g.* beginner, deterred, recurring.

(iii) The final consonant of kidnap, worship, handicap, bias, fuel, dial is also doubled, as kidnapper, worshipping, handicapped, dialled, and refuelling.

(iv) Words ending in an 'I' following a single vowel usually double the 'I', *e.g.*

quarrel → quarrelling

signal	→	signalled
distil	→	distiller
appal	→	appalled
model	→	modelling
repel	→	repellent

English has inherited this characteristics from its mother Sanskrit.

(i) In Sanskrit, a consonant followed by a vowel is doubled. Examples are :

pac	→	*papāca*
jāgṛ	→	*jajāgāra*
bhū	→	*babhūva*
gam	→	*jagām*
dā	→	*dadāti*

Cf. Pāṇ (6.1.1) *ekāco dve prathamasya.*

(ii) Sometimes a consonant preceded by a vowel is also doubled.

Examples are :

aṭ	→	*aṭiṭiṣati*
śiṣ	→	*asisiṣati*
riṣ	→	*aririṣati, etc.*

Cf. Paṇ. (6.1.72) *ajāderdvitīyasya.*

(iii) This doubling is also seen with regard to vowels. Examples are :

i	→	*iyāya*
ṛ	→	*āra*

English also exhibits this type of tendency in the following examples. eel, eerie, aardvark, aardwolf, aaron's-beard. *etc.*

7. *Inflection* : (1) Sanskrit employs *am* affix in the accusative sg. Case, *e.g.*

kim	→	*kam*
asmad	→	*mām*
tad	→	*tam*
Rāma	→	*Rāmam, etc.*

German has also inherited the same characteristics. It adds *am* in the form of 'em', *e.g.*

mein	→	meinem
sein	→	seinem
unser	→	unserem
ihr	→	ithem
der	→	dam
wer	→	wem

Though English has dropped accusative formations, it preserves 'whom' an accusative form of 'who' where it uses the same affix *am* as 'm'.

(ii) In Sanskrit, nominative plurals are formed with affix *s* or *āsas* (peculiar to Vedic Skt.), as in *Rāma*→*Rāmas*→ *Rāmāsas.* Similarly English forms its plural with 's' or 'es', *e.g.*

book	→	books
boy	→	boys
army	→	armies

(iii) The termination of genitive singular, dual and plural in Sanskrit are as (*ṅas*), *os* and *ām* respectively. European languages borrowed these termination as 'es' and 'os' for their possessive (genitive) case. By the time of the modern English, the sounds 'e' and 'o' of 'es' and 'es' were omitted and the omission was indicated by the apostrophe-sign ('). Hence, in English we have possessive forms like boy's. etc., etc.

8. *Prepositions or prefixes* : Prefixes are always employed in conjunction with verbs. In Vedic Sanskrit, they are employed indifferently after a verb as well as before it. They may be separated from the verb by some intervening word or words. For instance, in *nisasāda dhṛtavrato varuṇaḥ pastyāsvā* (*RV.* 1.25.10), the prefix *ā* is used after the verb *nisasāda*. In *vedā me adhyāsate* (*RV.* 1.25.9), the prefix *adhi* is used before the verb *āsate*. And in *indra vāyu ime sutā upa prayobhirāgatam* (RV. 1.2.4), the prefix *upa* is separated from the verb *āgatam*.

But Classical Sanskrit attests no such liberty regarding the application of prefixes. It adopts a fixed pattern in their use and always employs them immediately before a verb.[1] On the other hand, German follows Vedic Sanskrit and employs them after and before a verb and also separates them from the verb as the need be, *e.g.*

fahren 'to go'

ap fahren 'to leave, to depart'

(i) Ich *fahre* heute abend um 7 uhr *ap*. 'I leave at 7 this morning'

(ii) Sie *ruft* die texizentrale *an*. 'She calls up the texi-driver.'

(iii) Herr Fuchs *Kommt* um 10 uhr 20 in Frankfurt *an*. 'Mr. Fuccs arrives at 12.20 in Frankfurt.'

(iv) *Rufer* Sie bitte Herren Beuemann *an*. 'Please call Mr. Baumann up'

But English restricts the use of prefixes (prepositions) only after verbs.

They are used immediately after a verb or sometimes with the intervention by a word or words, *e.g.*

(i) The gun *went off* by itself.

(ii) He *went through* the whole book, but he couldn't discover anything new in it.

(iii) He *called* me *up*, etc., etc.

9. *Degrees of comparison* : In the Sanskrit language, the

---

[1] Cf. Pān. *te prāgdhāto* (1.4.80).

suffixes *-tara* and *-īyas* form the comparative degree and the suffixes *-tama* and *-iṣṭha* are employed to form the superlative degree.

These suffixes of comparison are retained in the European languages with slight variations. English borrows only *-iṣṭha* for superlative degree and *-tara* for comparative degree via other I.E. languages, *e.g.* Avesta retains the suffix *-iṣṭha* as *-'ista'*, Greek as -'iotas' and Gothic as 'ista'. Modern German retains this suffix as 'ste', *e.g.*

klein	-	kleinste
hoch	-	höchste
teuer	-	teuerste, etc.

English, too, under the influence of German retains *-iṣṭha* as '-est, thus

high	-	highest
noble	-	noblest, etc.

On the other hand, *-tara* is retained in latin as '-tru'; in Gothic as 'thara'; Old High German retains it as 'der'; in Middle German it is retained as '-der' and in Modern German, it reduced to '-er', thus

hoch	-	höher
teuer	-	teurer
klein	-	kleiner, etc.

English, too, following German retains Skt. *-tara* as -'er', *e.g.*

high	-	higher
low	-	lower, etc.[1]

Origin of English Months

Romans owe to Indians for the development of their

---

[1] For details see the author (Arya Ravi Prakash, 2007 : Part 1, Chap. 4)

calendar system. According to the author of *India in Greece* (P.142), 'Both among Greeks and Romans - the descendants of colonists from India, continued, specially amongst the latter people down to and throughout the most historical periods.' Thus the Vedic emigrants in Rome totally forget this division of zodiac in 12 parts. They used to count 10 months in a year and left some days uncounted. They begin with a fresh year with full moon in spring season as was in their memory. The names of their months were still driven from their original language, the Sanskrit such as *unus* from Sanskrit *eka*, *duo* from Sanskrit *dvau*, *tria* from Sanskrit *traya*, *quinque* from *pañca*, *sex* from Sanskrit *ṣaṭ*, *septem* from *sapta*, *octo* from *aṣṭau*, *noven* from Sanskrit *navan* and *decem* from Sanskrit *daśam*. The presently extant names of months like September, October, November and December clearly substantiate this fact. According to the Indian *Saurmān* system, *i.e.* the solar measurement of time, the sun passes through the twelve zodiac signs in a year and its passing through each sign makes a month. These 12 zodiac signs were known as 12 *ambers/rāsis* or stars and as result, the names of months were formed after suffixing ambar/amber to the numbers. With the passage of time, first six months were renamed either after some historical personalities or some specific historical events, though the last four months survived in their original form signalling their very origin to Sanskrit.

The Romanian calendar consisting of 10 months beginning from March as its first month upto December as its last month remained in vogue till 452 BC, when Numa Pompilius introduced the custom of inserting 23 days at the interval of two years. But the introduction of 23 days became the bone of contention among the heads of religious sects. This was at last removed by Julius Caesar who with the help of Cleopatra, the empress of Egypt reformed the Romulian calendar after the fashion of Egyptian calendar. This reform was known as Julian reform or Julian arrangement of calendar. The history goes like this :

Cleopatra was the empress of Egypt. She was Greek by birth and belonged to the dynasty founded by Tolami, a commander of Alexander. Following the death of Alexander,

Tolami declared his domain over Egypt. Clepatra was from his dynasty. She was born in 3033 kali era or 68 BC. Following the death of her father Tolami, the 11th, she took over the reign of Egypt along with her brother Tolami, the 12th. But she was over-thrown by her brother in the war of succession. She formed an army in Cypress and tried to recapture power. In the meantime, defeated by Caesar and fled to Egypt a brave soldier named Pompy was guillotined by Tolamy. With the view to please Caesar he (Tolami) presented his body to Caesar, but Caesar got annoyed at this. Meanwhile, to make a good use of the event, Cleopatra hiding herself in the precious carpets purchased by Romans met Caesar and he was also taken in by her exquisite beauty. He captured the regime from Tolami and handed it over to Cleopatra. Afterwards, both Caesar and Cleopatra roamed about the banks of the river Nile for many weeks. Cleopatra gave birth to a child who was named as Caesarian, i.e. Junior Caesar. When the queen of Egypt started domiciliating the palace of Rome as a queen-dowager, the artisans, economists and astrologers were sent for from Alexanderia, the capital of Egypt. Roman taxation system was reformed and a new currency was introduced. Roman calendar was also amended by dividing whole year into 365 days and by adding two more months to the already existing 10 months, after the fashion of Egyptian calendar. Since the time of Julius Caesar (46 BC), the Roman used to have 12 months with the new year commencing with March as the first *amber* (month).

March continued to be the beginning or the legal year in England until 18th century. In France, it was reckoned as the first month of the year until 1564, when by an edict of Charles IX, January was decreed to be the first month, so that the year may end with December, the months of Jesus Christ's birth. Scotland followed the example of France.[1]

The history goes further and we are told that during this arrangement, the quintiles amber (fifth month of Romulian calendar and the seventh month of Julian arrangement) was named July by the Egyptian astronomers to felicitate Julius

---

[1] See *Encyclopaedia Britannica,* Vol. 14. P. 866.

Caesar, as he was born on 12th of this month. This month was also assigned highest 31 days, since Caesar was the most powerful king of Rome. On the other hand, Caesar also, in turn, felicitated Cleopatra by constructing a temple of goddess of Venus. Illuckily, Caesar died after two years in 44 BC and Cleopatra had to return to her kingdom, Egypt.

Later Julius Augustus also named the sixth amber (sixtilis) after his name as August and also assigned 31 days to his month, since he considered himself no less brave than Julius Caesar.

Similarly, the first amber was named as Mars or March after the god of war. Actually, this was not only the beginning of the year, but was the open spring season for waging war. That was why, it was named after Mars, the god of war. 'Mars being the powerful god was also assigned 31 days.

The second *amber,* April, was named after Latin aperire 'to open' in allusion to its being the season when trees and flowers begin to 'open' and is supported by comparison with the modern Greek word 'opening' for spring. It was given fourth place in Julian calendar.

The third *amber* was named Maius by Romulus in respect to the senators and nobles of his city, who were called Majores. Being associated with Majores, it was also given 31 days. It became the fifth in Julian calendar, which later came to be known as May.

The fourth *amber* was called Junius in honour of the youths of Rome (i.e. Juniares) who served Romulus in war. Since it represented minors, it was assigned 30 days. Junius later came to be known as June.

September, October, November and December have come down to us in their actual form.

Januarius (January) and Februarius (February) were added at the end as 11th and 12th *amber* of the series by Numa Pompilius. Though in Julian arrangement their place was changed otherwise and they were considered to be the first and second months of the year, but in practical sense they still continue to be the last months. Since all the additions and subtractions are made to the last member of the series, Feb., being the last one, always adds a day in case of a leap year. These last two months were called January and February, because they wanted the year to end with December to facilitate the birth of Jesus Christ as before. As such the year was started with the newly added last two months only. January, in fact, originated from the Roman term *Janus* which is the corrupt form of Ganesh of Sanskrit. Ganesh symbolises the beginning of every act in Indian tradition, so following the same Indian tradition, Romans started their year with January formed from *Janus*. The next month was coined as Februarius which is the corrupt form of *pravara* of Sanskrit. *Pravara* also symbolises the first of sages born on the earth. On the same pattern, the term Februarius represented the lord of sages.

From the foregoing discussion it can unhesitatingly be inferred that all the English months can be traced back to Sanskrit via Greek, Roman and Egyptian ones.

Conclusion

On the basis of the foregoing discussion, it can be inferred that the origin of English can be traced back to Sanskrit traditionally via other European languages. Actually, all of the European languages find their prototypes directly or indirectly in Sanskrit.

The close affinity of European languages with Sanskrit will also help theorise the idea that the Vedic language speaking people must have emigrated from India to colonise alien lands and in course they must have shaped or modified the idiom of the dialects of alien inhabitants.

As regards the origin of the other languages of globe, it can be maintained that if a consistent thorough integrated research is carried out, all of them can also be traced back to Sanskrit traditionally via other cognate languages.

Thus, Sanskrit was the link language of the world over before long and still it has the capacity to link the whole world with one stirring of language and these days with the emergence of a new era of computer science, Sanskrit is proving to be the most fit, suitable and scientific language for computer purposes. Hence, the utility of Sanskrit is beyond doubt and now Sanskrit is the demand of time as well as clime.

Appendix- 1

English Vs. Tuḷu Vs. Sanskrit

By the end of 1987, the present author accomplished the task of establishing cognate words between Sanskrit and English and deduced the results that English originated from Sanskrit traditionally via other European languages. But with the beginning of 1988, he all of a sudden, came across a startling news heading 'English Traced to Origins of Speech' in one of the leading English dailies 'The Hindustan Times'. According to the paper, an Indian scholar Mr. P.S. Rai submitted a thesis on 'The Primary Evolution of human speech and a million year old English' to the Chairman, Department of linguistics, State University of New York, Dr. Mark Aronoff in October 1987. The paper reported that Mr. Rai established over 700 cognate words in Tuḷu and English vocabularies in the said thesis. According to him, modern literary English can be traced back via Tuḷu, the language of the inhabitants of India's south-west coast with which it has striking similarities, to the very origins of human speech about a million tears or so ago.

The above news was really alarming to me, as it appeared to have rendered my whole labour worthless. I then, managed to acquire a Tuḷu-English Dictionary edited by Professor M. Mariappa Bhat and published by the University of Madras. I went through the whole dictionary to locate the so-called 700 cognate words reported to have been established by Mr. Rai, but it was all in vain. On the contrary, I could locate a large number of cognate words between Sanskrit and Tuḷu. Thus, led by the notion of doubtful authenticity of Mr. Rai's work, I wrote on 9.2.89 to Dr. Mark Aronoff, the chairman Dept. of Linguistics, State University of New York, referring to the report of the said English daily and requested him to arrange me a photo-copy of the said thesis. On June 12, 1989 Dr. Aronoff replied to my query. I quote hereunder the exact version of his letter.

Dear Dr. Arya,

I am sorry to have delayed so long in responding to your letter. In any case. I have no positive news. Despite what you may have read, Mr. Rai did not submit any formal thesis to me. Mr. Rai and I spent an hour or so discussing his ideas, which I did not find to be proven, although admittedly this is not my area of greatest expertise. As far as I know, Mr. Rai's ideas have not been published elsewhere.

Sincerely yours.
Sd/
Mark Aronoff

Professor and Chairman

This information confirmed my doubts and I was all set to make further investigations about the relationship of Sanskrit and Tuḷu. On comparing the vocabularies of Sanskrit and Tuḷu, I came to know that Tuḷu has drawn a large number of vocables from Sanskrit. A couple of them may be illustrated hereunder.

Tuḷu vocables as drawn from Sanskrit

	Tulu	Sanskrit
1.	Pañcakajjāyo 'a sweet preparation made with five ingredients'	*Pañcakāt jāyaḥ*
2.	tāri 'tree'	*taru*
3.	paggu 'the first tuḷu month'	*phālgun*
4.	etāsti 'exact'	*yathāsthiti*
5.	kai 'hand'	*kara*
6.	ejño 'sacrifice'	*yajña*
7.	ekke 'a kind of a milk plant whose flower is sacred to lord 'Śiva'	*arka*
	Tulu	**Sanskrit**
8.	batti 'stick'	*varti*

9. kāmale 'jaundice'	*kāmalā*
10. ūno 'deficient'	*ūna*
11. urdi 'increase'	*vṛddhi*
12. niru 'water'	*nārā, nīra*
13. unguto 'the great toe'	*aṅguṣṭha*
14. uṅgilo 'a ring'	*aṅgulīyaka*
15. uṇasu 'a meal', 'dinner'	*aśana*
16. utpatti 'produce'	*utpatti*
17. upāso 'fast'	*upavāsa*
18. udāraṇa 'example'	*udāharaṅa*
19. kelu 'time'	*kāla*
20. iṭṭige 'side'	*iṣṭakā*
21. taṭṭu 'side'	*taṭa*
22. āpattu 'calamity, illness'	*āpatti*
23. āspāsu 'vicinity'	*āpārśva*
24. ākāso 'sky'	*ākāśa*

Hosts of similar other examples can be cited, but the paucity of time and space restrains the present author to detail all of them here.

Eventually, on the basis of Tuḷu borrowings from Sanskrit, it can safely be observed that the prototypes of Tuḷu forms are also preserved in the Sanskrit language.

Hence, it will be more beneficial and advisable to study the history of origin and development of various Indo-European and Dravidian languages with Sanskrit as their Proto-language.

Evolution of the Lithuanian Language

In Vedic Language forms with radical ending ī, accept a regular ending *-au* when inflected in nominative, accusative dual. But in the Vedic language regular ending *-au* is sometimes found replaced by *-ā* and sometimes found dropped altogether. For example in the forms of *nadyā* (nom. acc. dual of *nadī*) and *yamyā* (nom. acc. dual of *yamī*) -au is found replaced by -ā, but in the forms of *rodasī, devī, bṛhatī, pṛthivī, mahī, samicī* etc. it is found dropped altogether. (Arya, 2007 : 96) The same linguistic tendency can be recorded from Lithuanian that originated from Vedic Sanskrit. Lithuanian form of *Vezamtī* is found with the radical ending *-ī* by dropping the nom. acc. dual ending. (Arya, 2007 : Chapter 1, ft. 155).

Locative singular of Yuṣmad, second person pronoun, is *tvayi* and *tve. Tve* was predominantly used in the Vedic language, whereas *tvayi* occupied a dominant place in the later Vedic and Classical Sanskrit. (Arya, 2007 : 115). The Lithuanian following the pattern of Classical Sanskrit admitted *tvayi* as twiye. (Arya, 2007 : Chapter 2, ft. 81)

In addition to the above cited facts following list of borrowings in Lithuanian from Sanskrit shows its direct origin from Sanskrit, e.g.

Sanskrit	**Lithunain**
asmi (i am)	esmi
asi (you are)	essi
asti (he is)	esti
smaḥ (we are)	esmi
stha 'second person plural (You are)	esti
paśu (animal)	penss, pecku
go (cow)	gow
gau (bull)	govjado

Sanskrit	**Lithunain**
sthura (steer)	taura-s
aśva (horse)	aszua
avi (sheep)	avi-s
makṣikā (fly)	muse
eka (numeral denoting 'one')	wein
dvau (two)	du
tri (three)	tri
catur (four)	kettuar
pañc (five)	penki
ṣaṣ (six)	szestzi
sapta (seven)	septyni
aṣṭa (eight)	asztuni
nava (nine)	dewyni
daśa (ten)	deszimt
yuvoḥ (you two)	yumu, dwieyū
(Arya : 2007: 133: fn. 106),	
yuvam (Arya 2007: 132 : fn. 87)	yudu

Evolution of the Avestan Language

In Vedic Language forms radical ending *ī*, are accept a regular ending *-au* when inflected in nominative, accusative dual. But in the Vedic language regular ending *-au* is sometimes found replaced by *-ā* and sometimes found dropped altogether. For example in the forms of *nadyā* (nom. acc. dual of nadī) and yamyā (nom. acc. dual of yamī) *-au* is found replaced by *-ā*, but in the forms of *rodasī*, *devī*, *bṛhatī*, *pṛthivī*, *mahī*, *samicī* etc. it is found dropped altogether. (Arya, 2007 : 96) The same linguistic tendency can be recorded from Lithuanian that originated from Vedic Sanskrit. Avestan form of *Hamoistrī* is found with the radical ending *-ī* by dropping the nom. acc. dual ending. (Arya, 2007 : Chapter 1, ft. 155).

In Sanskrit, generally the stems ending in short vowel *ṛ* admit in genitive plural a euphonic n between the normal termination *-ām* and the stem. For example *pitṛṇām* (form *pitṛ*). But in the Vedic language, we found that this insertion has been dropped in a couple of cases. For example, *narām* (in place of *nṛṇām*) occurs 16 times in the *Ṛgveda*. *Svasrām* occurs once in the *Ṛgveda*. (Arya, 2007 : 97)The same tendency has percolated to Avesta also. There also the insertion of euphonic n between genitive case-ending and the stem has not been admitted. For instance, Sanskrit bhrātṛṇām becomes in Avesta as brathraṁm. (Arya, 2007 : Chapter 1, ft. 161). This shows that in the ealrier stages of the Vedic language, the tendency of inserting euphonic 'n' was less prevalent, but later it became more and more prevalent. Greek also exhibits the later tendency. This proves that Greek originated from Vedic Sanskrit when the later Vedic Sanskrit was evolving.

Tyad is a pronoun which was used in the Vedic language. It became obsolete in Classical Sanskrit. (Arya, 2007 : 109). The same pronoun was retained by Avesta as *thya* during the process of its evolution from Vedic Sanskrit. (Arya, 2007 : Chapter 2, ft. 4)

Ava is pronominal stem that was used scarcely even in the Vedas. Its use is not attested in later Vedic and Classical Sanskrit.

(Arya, 2007 : 110) Its use is registered in Avesta as ava. (Arya, 2007 : Chapter 2, ft. 11)

Locative singular of *Yuṣmad*, second person pronoun, is *tvayi* and *tve*. *Tve* was prediminantly used in the Vedic language, whereas tvayi occupied a dominant place in the later Vedic and Classical Sanskrit. (Arya, 2007 : 115) The Avesta following the pattern of Classical sanskrit admitted tvayi as thvahmi. (Arya, 2007 : Chapter 2, ft. 81)

Following is list of borrowings in Avestan from Sanskrit which speaks of its origin from Sanskrit, e.g.

Sanskrit	**Avesta**
asmi (I am)	almi
asi (you Are)	ahi
asti (he is)	asti
smaḥ (we are)	hualie
stha (you are)	sta
pitṛ (father)	patar
mātṛ (mother)	matar
bhrātṛ (brother)	brator
Duhitṛ (daughter)	dighdhar
paśu (animal)	pasu
go (cow)	gao
ukṣan (bull)	ukhshan
sthura (steer)	staoru
aśva (horse)	aspa
makṣikā (fly)	makshki

In addition to the above cognates, correspondence between the following numerals (ordinal numbers) also proves that Avesta is none else but the corrupt form of Sanskrit only.

prathamam (first)	frat'hema

dvitīya (second)	bitya
tṛtīya (third)	thritya
caturtha, *turīya* (fourth)	turiya
pañcama (fifth)	pugdha
ṣaṣṭha (sixth)	cstva
saptam (seventh)	haptat'ha
aṣṭama (eighth)	astema
navam (ninth)	nauma
daśam (tenth)	dasema

Following analogy of verbs between Sanskrit and Avesta is revealing :

dad-a-mi (I give)	dadha-mi
dada-s (you give)	dadh-si
dada-te (he gives)	dadha-te
dadmaḥ (we give)	dade-mahi
dat-tha (you give)	dasta
dad-te (they give)	dade-nti

Avesta could also retain personal terminations of its source language Sanskrit while emerging as a separate language. Following examples are noteworthy :

tiṣṭhāmi (I stay)	histami
dadami (I give)	dadhami
asmi (I am)	ahmi
vahami (I carry)	vazami
bharami (I bear)	barami

asi (you are)	ahi
tiṣṭhasi (you stay)	hisht'hahi
dadasi (you give)	dadhahi
bharasi (you bear)	barahi
tiṣṭhathas (you two stay)	histois
bhares (you carry)	bharois
tiṣṭhatha (you all stay)	hist'hat'ha
bharatha (you all bear)	bara'ha
dadyāt (he should give)	daidhyata
bhareta (he should bear)	baraeta
asti (he is)	ashti
tiṣṭhati (he stays)	hishtoti
dadāti (he gives)	dadhaite
bharati (he bears)	baraite
bharet (he should bear)	baroit
dadyāt (he should give)	daidhyat
santi (they are)	hente
tiṣṭhanti (they stay)	histenti
dadati (they give)	dadenti
bharanti (they bear)	barenti
vahanti (they carry)	vazenti

The aforementioned examples prove beyond any shadow of doubt that Avesta finds its proto-type in Sanskrit. The above fact has also been corroborated by the findings of William Jones (Sir William Jines' works, Vol.1, pp.82-83) following remarks. he says, 'I was not little surprised to find that out of ten words in Du Peron's Zind Dictionary six or seven out of ten words were pure Sanskrit.' In view of the above fact, Prof. Heeren (Historical Researches, Vol. ī, p.20) had to declare that 'In point of fact, the Zind is derived from Sanskrit.' Thus the affinity of European languages and Old Parsi with Sanskrit and use of cognate idioms by these languages proves that the nations who used them must have descended from Indian stock.

Evolution of the Greek Language

In Sanskrit, generally the stems ending in short vowel *'ṛ'* admit in genitive plural a euphonic *'n'* between the normal termination *-ām* and the stem. For example *pitṛṇām* (form *pitṛ*). But in the Vedic language, we found that this insertion has been dropped in a couple of cases. For example, *narām* (in place of *nṛṇām*) occurs 16 times in the *Ṛgveda*. *Svasrām* occurs once in the *Ṛgveda*. (Arya, 2007 : 97). The same tendency has percolated to Greek also. There also the insertion of euphonic '*n*' between genitive case-ending and the stem has been admitted and the genitive case-ending *-ām* has been admitted as -on (ωυ). For instance, Sanskrit *bhrātṛṇām* becomes in Greek as παιερωυ . (Arya, 2007 : Part 2, Chapter 1, ft. 161) . This shows that in the earlier stages of the Vedic language, the tendency of inserting euphonic 'n' was less prevalent, but later it became more and more prevalent. Greek also exhibits the later tendency. This proves that Greek originated from Vedic Sanskrit when the later Vedic Sanskrit was evolving.

Although students of both Greek and Latin may be impressed with their similarities, Latin does not have a dual number, a middle voice, or an aorist tense, which both Greek and Sanskrit share. These features, and others, prove that Latin originated from Sanskrit very late as compared to Greek.

Following are some of the borrowings in Greek from Sanskrit which speaks of its origin from Sanskrit, e.g.

Sanskrit	**Greek**	**Meaning in English**
1. *tānam*	tonom	tone
2. *paru*	pur	fire
3. *pardate*	bdeetai	farteth (fart)
4. *puras*	paros	fore

Sanskrit	**Greek**	**Meaning in English**
5. *fullam*	phullon	flower
6. *phavate*	phvetai	beeth,
7. *bhrū*	ophrus	brow
8. *madhu*	methu	mead
9. *manate*	mnaetai	meaneth
10. *mahatva*	megethos	might
11. *me*	me	me
12. *roṣa*	orgç	rage
13. *rohita*	ereuthon	red
14. *vakṣate*	aezetai	waxeth
15. *vepate*	uphaetai	weaveth
16. *śāla*	skholç	school
17. *hanum*	genuu	chin
18. *ajra 'plain'*	ager	acre, agriculture
19. *trikoṇamiti*	trigonov	trignometry
20. *takṣaka*	töeikhov	tonic
21. *ātma, aṇu*	atomas	atom
22. *amṛta*	immortal	immortle

Evolution of the Latin

In Sanskrit, generally the stems ending in short vowel *ṛ* admit in genitive plural a euphonic n between the normal termination -ām and the stem. For example *pitṛṇām* (form *pitṛ*). But in the Vedic language, we found that this insertion has been dropped in a couple of cases. For example, narām (in place of nṛṇām) occurs 16 times in the *Ṛgveda. Svasrām* occurs once in the Ṛgveda. (Arya, 2007 : 97)The same tendency has percolated to Latin also. There also the insertion of euphonic n between genitive case-ending and the stem has not been admitted and the genitive case-ending -ām has been admitted as -um. For instance, Sanskrit *bhrātṛṇām* becomes in Latin as fratr-um. (Arya, 2007 : Part, 2 Chapter 1, ft. 161). This shows that in the ealrier stages of the Vedic language, the tendency of inserting euphonic '*n*' was less prevalent, but later it became more and more prevalent. Greek also exhibits the later tendency. This proves that Greek originated from Vedic Sanskrit when the later Vedic Sanskrit was evolving.

Locative singular of *yuṣmad*, second person pronoun, is tvayi and tve. *Tve* was predominantly used in the Vedic language, whereas tvayi occupied a dominant place in the later Vedic and Classical Sanskrit. (Arya, 2007 : 115) Latin following the pattern of Classical Sanskrit admitted *tvayi* as *tvi.* (Arya, 2007 : Chapter 2, ft. 81)

Latin does not have a dual number, a middle voice, or an aorist tense, which both Greek and Sanskrit share. These features, and others, prove that Latin indirectly originated from Vedic Sanskrit very late as compared to Greek.

Following list of borrowings in Latin from Sanskrit also speaks of Latin's origin from Sanskrit, e.g.

Sanskrit	Latin	Meaning in English
1. *tarman*	terminus	term
2. *tānam*	tonum	tone

Sanskrit **Latin** **Meaning in English**

3. *naddham*	nodum	knot
4. *pardate*	pedit	farteth (fart)
5. *puras*	prae	fore
6. *prānta*	frontem	front
7. *fullam*	folium	flower
8. *phavate*	fuit	beeth
9. *manate*	monet	meaneth
10. *me*	me	me
11. *mitam*	metitum	meted
12. *mṛtam*	mortuum	mortal
13. *yat*	id	it
14. *yuvan*	juvenis	young
15. *lapana*	labium	lip
16. *locayati*	lucet	lixeth (A.S.)
17. *vakṣate*	auget	waxeth
18. *varāhaḥ*	verses	boar, bare (A.S.)
19. *vastyayati*	vastat	wasteth
20. *śāla*	schola	school
21. *śṛnga*	cornu	horn
22. *santaḥ*	sanctus	saint
23. *siwati*	suit	seweth
24. *sīdati*	cedet	cedeth
25. *svanitam*	sonitum	sound

Evolution of Old Slav. and other Slavic languages

Locative singular of *yuṣmad*, second person pronoun, is *tvayi* and *tve*. *Tve* was predominantly used in the Vedic language, whereas *tvayi* occupied a dominant place in the later Vedic and Classical Sanskrit. (Arya, 2007 : 115) Old Slav. following the pattern of Classical Sanskrit admitted *tvayi* as 'tebye'. (Arya, 2007: Chapter 2, ft. 81). In addition to this, Slavic languages evolved the comparison of the following Slavic terms with that of Sanskrit gives one to understand the deep rooted relationship of Slavic languages with Sanskrit and

Following borrowings in Slavic languages from Sanskrit speaks of their origin from Sanskrit, e.g.

Sanskrit	**Meaning in English**	**Slovenian**	**Czech**	**Russian**
Words associated with water, moisture and other liquids				
megha	cloud	Megla	mlha (fog)	mgla (gloom)
Mṛṣ, marṣati	to sprinkle, pour out	Mršèati	mziti	marasit'
pa, papīyat	to quaff, drink intox. Liquors	Popivati	popijeti	zapit'
pa, pāyayati	cause to drink	Pojiti	(na)pájeti	poit'
pa, pibati	to drink, quaff	Piti	píti	pit'
Phena	foam, froth, saliva	Pena	pìna	Pena
Piti	drinking	Pitje	pití	pit'io
plavana	swimming, floating	Plavanje	plavání	plavan'e
plu, plavate	to swim, float	Plavati	plavati	plavat'
Rasa	moisture, humidity, any liquid	rosa (dew)	rosa	rosa (dew)

Sanskrit	Meaning in Englsh	Slovenian	Czech	Russian
Salila	tears	Solze	slzy	Sliozy
salilavat	provided with water	Zalivan	zalívan	Zalityy
sarasa	a lake, pond	Jezero	jezero	Ozero
sna, snasyati	to bathe, wash, cleanse	Snažiti	x	X
uda,am	water	voda (also: uda)	voda	Voda
voda, udanya	moist	Voden	vodní	X
varṣ & pruṣṇoti	to rain, shower down	Pršiti	pršeti	marasit'
apuplavat	to inundate, to submerge	Poplaviti	zaplaviti	
Varya	watery, aquatic	barje, bara		

Words associated with food, food preparation and consumption

ad, atsyati	to eat	jesti	jísti	yest'
adanīya	to be eaten, what may be eaten	jeden	jídlo	s'ieden
Adya	food	jed	jídlo	yeda
cuṣati	to suck	cuzati, sesati	cucati	sosat'
cuṣana	sucking	cuzanje	cucání	sosanie'
Dhe, dhayati	to give suck, nourish	dojiti	dojiti (animal)	doit'
gavyaya	coming from cattle	goveje	hovadina	goviadina
gavyaya yuṣa	beef soup	goveja juha	x	goviazhia yushka
ghas,-ati	to consume or devour, eat	gostiti se, kositi	pásti se (graze)?	x
Ghasi	food	Kaša	x	kasha

Sanskrit	Meaning in Englsh	Slovenian	Czech	Russian
Ghasa	food, meadow or pasture grass	Koša	kosení	X
Jeh, jehate	be thirsty; to open the mouth	žejati; zehati, zevati	žíznit	zhazhdat'; zevat
Jivatu	victuals, food	Živež	x	X
kośa, koṣa	vessel, box, bucket, store-room	koš, košara	koš	Kovsh
koṣṭaka	granary, store-room	Kašèa	x	X
Kṣīra	milk, thickened milk	sir (cheese)	syr	syr (cheese)
kuṣ,-ati; kuṣ,-ṇāti	to gnaw, nibble; to test	(po)kušati; skušati	pokoštova ti:skoušet skoušet	kushat'; x
Mas	flesh, meat; month	meso; mesec	maso: mesíc	miaso; miesiats
mekṣaṇa	stick or spoon for stirring	Mešalka	méchaèka	Meshalka
mikṣ, mekṣayati	to stir up, mix, mingle	Mešati	míchatí	meshat'
pa, pibati/ papīyat	to drink	Piti	pítí	pit'
pac-ati	to bake, cook	Peèi	peèi	pech'
pacana	cooking, roasting	Peèenje	peèeni	Pechenyi
Paktri	one who bakes or roasts	Pek	pekaø	pekar'
pāpacyate	to cook very much, burn	Popeèi	pøepéci	popech'

Sanskrit	Meaning in Englsh	Slovenian	Czech	Russian
papīti	mutual or reciprocal drinking	popivanje	popíjení	x
pīta	food, nourishment	pièa	x	pishcha
Pita	saturated, filled with	pitan	x	napitan
pūrṇa	Filled, full, abundant	poln	plny	polon, polnyi
sūpa	soup, broth	župa	x	sup
yemana=j emana	Eating	jemati (zdravilo)	x	x
Words associated with death, pain and pleasure				
bal,-ate	to hurt; to expound	boleti	boleti	bolet'
bharts-ayati	to abuse, to pain	brcati	x	
du, davayati	to cause pain, sorrow	daviti	x	davit'(to press)
kaṣ-ati	to scrape, hurt, destroy	kaziti	kazit	kaznit'(execute)
klath-ati	To hurt, kill	klati	x	kolot'
Kṛcchara	causing trouble, pain	krè (cramp)	x	x
krudha	harsh, cruel	krut	kruty	x
Kruś, krośati	to cry out, shriek	krièati	krièet	krichat'
math-ati	to trouble, disturb	motiti	x	mutit'
mṛ, maryate	to kill, slay	moriti	x	morit'
mṛ, mriyate/ marate	to die, decease	mreti, umirati	umirat	umirat'
mṛc, marcayati	to hurt, injure	mrcvariti	x	x

Sanskrit	Meaning in Englsh	Slovenian	Czech	Russian
Mṛta	dead, rigid, torpid	Mrtev	mrtevt	Miortv
Mṛyu	dying, death	mrtje=mret je, smrt	umirati, smrt	sm'ert'
Mṛtaka	dead man, corpse	Mrtvak	mrtvola,m rtvelec	m'ertv'ets
pratap-ayati	to destroy, torment	Pretepati	trapit	X
ru, rauti	to roar, cry outloud	Rjuti	rvat	orat'
ru, ravate	to break, kill	Ruvati	x	rubit'
rup, ropayat	to cause violent pain	ropati (plunder)	x	X
ruṣ,-ati	to hurt, injure, kill	rušiti (destroy)	rušit	rushit (destroy)
vraṇ,ati	to wound	Raniti	ranit	ranit'
vraṇa	Wound	Rana	rana	Rana
vunt-ayati	to kill, hurt	Fentati	x	X

Verb 'to be'

Asmi	I am	Sem	jsem	X; yesm' (archaic) (archaic0 (archaic)
Asi	you are	Si	jsi	X; yesi (archaic)
Asti	he, she, it is	x (je)	x (je)	Yest
svaḥ	X	Sva	x	X
sthaḥ	X	sta	x	X
staḥ	X	Sta	x	X
smaḥ	we are	smo	jsme	X; (yest)
Stha	you are	Ste	jste	X; (yest)
Santi	they are	x (so)	x (jsou)	X; (yest)
Numerals				
Eka	One	eden:neki (someone) (neki) (someone)	nějaký (someone)	Odin

Sanskrit	Meaning in Englsh	Slovenian	Czech	Russian
dvi (dva)	Two	Dva	dva	dva
Tri	Three	Tri	tøi	tri
Catur	Four	štiri (èetveri)	ètýøi	chetyre
pañc	Five	pet	pét	piat'
ṣaṣ, ṣaṭ	Six	Šest	šest	shest'
Saptan	Seven	sedem	sedm	siem'
Aṣṭan	Eight	osem	osm	vasiem'
Navan	Nine	devet	devét	dieviat'
daśan	Ten	deset	deset	diesiat'
ekādaśan	Eleven	enajst	jedenáct	odinnadsat'
Dvadaśan	Twelve	dvanajst	dvananáct	dvenadsat'
śata	hundred	Sto	sto	sut', sto

From the above comparison, it can be seen that Slovenian has preserved more general vocabulary of Sanskrit than other Slavic languages such as Czech and Russian that is common to Sanskrit. In some cases, Slovenian still preserves vocabulary and grammatical forms no longer used in Indian languages such as Hindi and Punjabi. The conjugation of the verb *to be* is a good example.

Slovenian has also kept the meaning of the words quite close to the Vedic Sanskrit, along with the sounds. The greatest similarity is with the Vedic Sanskrit - the language of the Vedas.

Vedic Origin of Numbers in the World Languages

Numerals in all the world languages find their origin directly or indirectly from Sanskrit. Following comparison of numerals of world languages with that of Sanskrit proves this fact.

Chart 1 (Numerals from No.1 to No. 5)

Languages	No.1	No. 2	No.3	No.4	No.5
Vedic or Indo European Error! Bookmark not defined. Sanskrit	ekaḥ/ ekas	dvau	trayas	catvāraḥ/ catvaras	*pañ-ca
Germanic					
Old Germanic+	*ainaz	*twai	*thrijiz	*fithwor	*fimfi
Western					
Old English+	án	twá	þrí	féower	fîf
Middle English+	an	two	three	four	fif
English	one	two	three	four	five
Scots	ane	twa	thrie	fower	fyve
Old Frisian+	en	twe	thre	fiuwer	fif
W.Frisian	ien	twa	trije	fjouwer	fiif
Frisian (Saterland)	aan	twæi	træi	fjauer	fieuw
Dutch	een	twee	drie	vier	vijf
W/S Flemish	ièn	twiè	drie	viere	vuvve
Brabants	iën	twië	draë	vi:r	vaìf
Low Saxon	een	twee	dree	veer	fief
Emsland	*e*in	tw*e*i	dr*e*i	f*e*iæ	fi:f
Mennonite Plautdietsch	een	twee	dree	fea	fief

Afrikaans	een	twee	drie	vier	vyf
German	eins	zwei	drei	vier	fýnf
Central Bavarian	oans	zwoa	drai	viare	fimbfe
Swabian	oes	zwoe	droe	vier	fýmf
Alsatian	eins	zwei	drëi	vier	fenf
Cimbrian	òan	zbeen	drai	viar	výf
Rimella	ais	zwai	drei	viére	venve
Rheinfränkisch	ääns	zwei	drej	vir	fennef
Pennsylvania	eens	zwee	drei	vier	fimf
Luxembourgeois	eent	zwee	dräi	véier	finnef
Swiss German	eis	zwei	drüü	vier	foif
Yiddish	eyns	tsvey	dray	fir	finef
Middle High German+	ein	zwe:ne	dri:e	vier	fýnf
Old High German+	ein	zwâ	drî	fior	fimf
Northern					
Runic+	æinn	tvæiR	þri:R	fiu:riR	fȲ:m
Old Norse+	einn	tveir	thrír	fjórir	fimm
Norwegian	en (*Ny.* ein)	to	tre	fire	fem
Danish	én	to	tre	fire	fem
Swedish	en	två	tre	fyra	fem
Faroese	ein	tveir	tríggir	fy'ra	fimm
Old Icelandic+	einn	tueir	þrír	fiórer	fimm
Icelandic	einn	tveir	þrír	fjórir	fimm
Eastern					
Gothic+	ains	twai	þreis	fidwor	fimf
Crimean+	ene	tua	tria	fyder	fyuf
Italic					

Oscan+	uinus	dus	tris	petora	pompe-
Umbrian+	uns	tuf	trif	petur-	pumpe-
Faliscan+		du	tris		*cuicue
Latin+	u:nus	duo	tre:s	quattuor	quinque
Romance					
Mozarabic+	uno	dox	trex	quatro	chinco
Portuguese	um	dois	três	quatro	cinco
Galician	un	dous	tres	catro	cinco
Spanish	uno	dos	tres	cuatro	cinco
Ladino	unu	do	tre	cuatru	sincu
Asturian	uno	dos	tres	cuatru	cincu
Aragonese	un	dos	tres	cuatro	zinco
Catalan	un	dos	tres	quatre	cinc
Valencian	u	dos	tres	quatre	cinc
Old French+	un	deus	treis	quatre	cinc
French	un	deux	trois	quatre	cinq
Walloon	onk	deus	troes	cwate	cênk
Jèrriais	ieune	deux	trais	quat'	chïnq
Poitevin	in	deùs	tràes	quatre	cênc
Old Picard+	ung	diaus	trois	katre	chincq
Picard	in	deu	trouo	kat	chink
Occitan (Provençal)	un	dos	tres	quatre	cinc
Lengadocian	un	dos	tres	quatre	cinc
Gascon	un	dus	tres	quate	cinc
Auvergnat	vun	dou	trei	catre	sin
Limosin	un	do:u:	trei	qua:tre	cin
Franco-Provençal (Vaudois)	on	doû	trâi	quatro	cin
Rumantsch	in	dus	trais	quatter	tschintg

Grischun					
Sursilvan	in	dus	treis	quater	tschun
Vallader	ün	duos	trais	quatter	tschinch
Friulian	u~ng	doy	tre	kwàtri	chingk
Ladin	un	doi	trëi	cater	cinc
Dalmatian+	join	doi	tra	kwatro	chenk
Italian	uno	due	tre	quattro	cinque
Piedmontese	ün	Dü	trè	quatr	sinc
Milanese	vun	duu	trii	quatter	cinqu
Genovese	un	doì	trei	quattro	èinque
Venetian	on	Do	tri	cuatro	sinque
Parmesan	von	Du	trì	cuatar	sinc
Corsican	unu	dui	trè	quattru	cinque
Umbrian	unu	dui	tre	quattru	cênque
Neapolitan	unë	rujë	tréië	quattë	cinghì
Sicilian	unu	dui	**tri**	qua**tt**ru	cincu
Romanian	unu	doi	trei	patru	cinci
Arumanian	unu	doi	trei	patru	**t**in**t**i
Meglenite	unu	doi	trei	patru	**t**in**t**i
Istriot	ur	doi	trei	påtru	**t**in**t**
Sardinian	unu	duos	tres	báttor	chimbe
Celtic					
Proto-Celtic+	oinos	dvai	treis	qetveres	qenqe
Gaulish+	*ônos	*duô	treis	petor	*pempe
Brythonic (P-Celtic)					
Welsh	un	dau	tri	pedwar	pump
Cardiganshire	în	Tô	târ	câr	cw^i
Breton	unan	daou	tri	pewar	pemp

Vannetais	unan	deu	tri	pear	pemp
Unified Cornish+	un	deu	try	peswar	pymp
Common	onan	dew	tri	peswar	pymp
Modern	on	deaw	try	pager	pemp
Devonian+	un	deu	tri	peduar	pemp
Goidelic (Q-Celtic)					
Old Irish+	óen	da	tri	ceth(a)ir	cóic
Irish	aon	dó	trí	ceathair	cúig
Scots Gaelic	aon	dà	trì	ceithir	cóig
Manx	nane	jees	tree	kiore	queig
Hellenic					
Mycenean Greek+	e-me (*hemei)	du-wo (*dwo)	ti-ri- (*tri-)	qe-to-ro (*q^{u}etro-)	
Classical Greek+	hei:s	dúo:	trei:s	téttares	pênte
Greek	éna	dhío	tría	téssera	pênde
Cypriot	énas	thkió	dris	désseris	bênde
Tsakonian	éna	dhíu	chía	tésera	pênde
Tocharian					
Tocharian A+	sas	wu	tre	s'twar	päü
Tocharian B+	se	wi	trai	s'twer	pis'
Albanian					
Albanian	një	dy	tre	katër	pesì
Gheg (Qosaj)	n'â	dy	tre	katër	pës
Tosk (Mandritsa)	ni	g'u	tri	kátrë	pêsì
Armenian					
+Classical Armenian	mi	erk'u	erek^h	chork^h	hing
Armenian	mek	yerku	yerek^h	chor^s	hing
Baltic					

West					
Old Prussian+	ai:ns	dwa:i	trijan	keturja:i	pe:nkja:i
East					
Lithuanian	víenas	dù	try~s	Keturì	penkí
Latvian	viêns	divi	trî:s	Chetri	píeci
Latgalian	vi:ns	divi	trejs	Chetri	pi:ci
Slavic					
East					
Russian	odín odín	dva dva	tri tri	ceti:re chety're	pÃth pyat'
Belarussian	adzín adzín	dva dva	try try	cati:ry chaty'ry	pÃthh piac'
Ukrainian	odín ody'n	dva dva	tri tri	Cotíri choty'ry	p'Ãth pyat'
West					
Polish	jeden	dwa	trzy	Cztery	pie,c'
Kashubian	jeden	dva	tr^ë	shtërë	pjin'c
Polabian+	janü	dåvo	tåri	citêr	pa,t
Czech	jeden	dva	tr^i	chtyr^i	pët
Slovak	jeden	dva	tri	shtyri	pät'
West	jeden	dva	try	shtyry	pet
East	jeden	dva	tri	shtyri	pejc
Upper Sorbian	jedyn	dwaj	tr^i	shtyri	pjec'
Lower Sorbian	jaden	dwa	ts'o	styrjo	pës'
South					
Old Church Slavonic+	jedinu	diva	trije	chetyre	pe,ti
Bulgarian	edín	dva	tri	chétiri	pet
Macedonian	eden	dva	tri	chetiri	pet
Serbo-Croat	jèdan	dvâ	trî	chètiri	pët

Slovene	ena	dva	tri	shtiri	pet
Anatolian					
Hittite+	*a:nt-	da:-	tri-	meiu-	
Luwian+	*a-	duwa-	*tarri-	*mawi-	*pa^{n}ku
Lycian+	sñta	tuwa	tri(ja)	teteri	
Indo-Iranian					
Iranian					
Eastern					
Ossetian Iron	iu	dIuuæ	ærtæ	tsIppar	fondz
Digor	ieu	duuæ	ærtæ	cuppar	fondz
Avestan+	ae:uua-	duua	thra:iio:	chathBa: ro:	pancha
Khwarezmian+	'yw	dhw	shy	cf'r	pnc
Sogdian+	'yw		dhry	chtf'r	panch
Yaghnobi	i:	du	siráu	tafó:r	panch
Bactrian+	io:go			sofaro	
Saka+	s's'au	duva	drai	tcahora	pa**m**jsa
Pashto	yaw	dwa	dre	tsalór	pindz^{ê}
Wakhi	i:	bu	tru	cybyr	pa:nz^{j}
Munji	yu	lu	sherai	chfu:r	pa:nj
Yidgha	yu	loh	shuroi	chshi:r	panj
Ishkashmi	uk	di,	ru,	ci,fu,r	pu,ndz
Sanglechi	vak	do:u	tra:i	safo:r	panz
Shughn	yi:w	dhu	aráy	cavó:r	pi:ndz
Rushani	yi:w	dhaw	aráy	cavú,r	pi:ndz
Yazgulami	wu,	dhow	cu,y	cher	penj
Sarikoli (Tashkorghani)	iw	dhew	aróy	cavúr	pindz
Parachi	zhu	Di	shi	cho:r	po:nc
Ormuri	so:	dyo:	sh.^{r}e:	tsa:r	pe:ndz

Western

Northwest

Parthian+	'yw	dw		cf'r	pnj
Yazdi	ya	Du	sey	chuhr	pänj
Nayini	yak			cha:or	penj
Natanzi	yæk	Do	se	chahar	pänj
Khunsari	yäg	Dô:	se	cha:r	pe:sh
Gazi	yeg	Dü	se	cha:r	ba:ng^
Sivandi	yä	Do	se	cha:r	päng^
Vafsi	yey	Do	se	caar	pezh
Semnani	i	Do	hejrá	cha:r	panj
Sangisari	yækæ'	d°o	shæ	chår	panj
Gilaki	y^{e}k	Du	se	chår	p^{e}nj
Mazanderani	yak	De	se	cha:r	panj
Talysh	i	Du	se	cho	penj
Harzani	i	De	here	chö	pinch
Zaza	zhew	Di	hi:re:	chihaa:r	pa:nzh
Gorani	yak	d'ue	y'are	chu'a:r	panj
Baluchi	y^{e}k	Do	s^{e}h	car	p^{e}nj
Turkmenistan	yak	Du	say	cha:r	panch
E Hill	yak	Do	sai	chiár	phanch
Rakhshani (Western)	y^{e}kk	dw	s^{e}y	char	p^{e}nch
Kermanji (S) Kurdish	yak	Du:	se:	chwa:r	pe:nj
Zaza (N) Kurdish	e:k	Dô	se:	cha:r	pe:nj
Bajalani	ikke:	Du:wa	sa	chwa:r	panj
Kermanshahi	yäkî'	dû'an	sî'an	chuâr	pänch
Southwest					
Old Persian+	aiva				*pancha

Pahlavi+	e:vak	do:	si:	chaha:r	panch
Farsi	yak	do	se	chaha:r	panj
Isfahani	ye(k)	do	se	tsâr	payn
Tajik	yak	du	se	chor	panj
Tati	yæ	dy"	sæ	char	panj
Chali	i	dö	sö	cua:r	panj
Fars	yek	do	se	chår	pänj
Lari	yak	do	se	ca:r	panj
Luri	ya	du	se	cha:r	panch
Kumzari	yek	doh	soh	cha:r	panj
Nuristani					
Ashkun	ach	d**o:**	trä	cata:	p**o:**nc
Wasi-weri	i pü:n	lü:	cshi:	ch^{i}pu:	wuchu
Kati	ev	d'u	tre	sht^{e}vo	puch
Kalasha-ala	ew	dü:	tre:	chata:	pu: ~
Indic					
Prakrit+	ekko:	do:	tao:	chatta:ri	paücha
Ardhamagadhi+	ege	do	tao	cattaro	pa**m**ca
Pali+	eka	dvi	ti	catu	paüca
Romany (Gypsy)					
Spanish	yes	duis	trin	sistar	parchen
Welsh	yek'	du:i:	trin	shto:r	pansh
Kalderash	yek(h)	duy	trin	shtar	panz'
Syrian	e:kâ	di:	târân	shta:r	Panj
Armenian	jäku	du:^{i}	t^{e}rín	ishdó:r	Bench
Iranian	yek	duy	terín	Ishta:r	pa:nj
Sinhalese-Maldivian					
Sinhalese	eka	deka	tuna	hatara	Paha

Vedda	ekamay	dekamay	tunamay	hataramay	pahamay
Maldivian	eke	de	tine	hatare	Fahe
Northern India					
Dardic					
Kashmiri	akh	zɨ	tr'ɨ	co:r	pa:nc
Shina	êk	du	**che**	char	poi ~
Brokskat	e:k	d̲u	t̲ra	ch^{h}or	Puns
Phalura	a:k	du:	tro:	chu:r	pa:nzh
Bashkarik	ak	du:	**t**ha:	cho:r	Panj
Tirahi	ek	do:	tre	cawo:r	Panc
Torwali	ek	du	cha	chau	Pan
Wotapuri	yek	du:	**t**a:	cawu:r	Panzh
Maiya	ak	du:	**t**ha:	saur	pa:nz
Kalasha	ek	du	tre	chau	**Poü**
Khowar	i	ju	troy	chhor	Ponj
Dameli	ek	du:	trâ	cho:r	pâ ~ ch
Gawar-bati	yok	du:	l^{y}e	cu:r	po:nc
Pashai	i:	do:	trä	cha:r	Panja
Shumashti	yäk	du:	l^{y}y	cöuur	po:n
Nangalami	yak	du:	**s**le:	ch^{u}or	Pa**n**
Dumaki	ek	dui	**c**ai	chouur	Poi
Western					
Marathi	ek	don	ti:n	char	pac
Konkani	êk	dôn	tin	char	panch
Sindhi	hiku	bba	**t**i:	ca:re	paüja
Khatri	hakro	bo	trê	chár	panj
Lahnda	hikk	do:e:	trä	cha:r	paü
Central					

Hindi/ Urdu	ek	do	ti:n	ca:r	pã:c
Parya	yek	do	tin	char	panj
Punjabi	yk	do	tyn	car	p^{e}üj
Siraiki	hik	du	tre	ca:r	paüj
Gujarati	ek	be	tr^{e}ñ	car	pãc
Rajasthani (Marwari)	e:k	do:y	ti:n	chya:r	pã:ch
Banjari (Lamani)	ek	di	tin	caar	paanc
Malvi	e:k	do:	ti:n	cha:r	pã:ch
Bhili	e:k	be:	te:n.	sya:r	pã:s
Dogri	ik	do:	trai	cha:r	paüj
Kumauni	e:k	dwi:	ti:n	cha:r	pã:ch
Garhwali	e:k	dwi:	ti:n	cha:r	pã:ch
W Pahari	e:k	dui	co:n	tsa:r	pa:ndz
Khandeshi	e:k	do:n	ti:n	cha:r	pa:ch
East Central					
Nepali	ek	dui	tin	cha:r	pa:nch
Maithili	ek	du:	ti:n	cha:ri	pã:ch
Magahi	ek	du:	ti:n	ca:r	pa:üc
Bhojpuri	e:k	dui	ti:n	ca:ri	pã:c
Awadhi (Kosali)	e:k	dui	ti:ni	ca:ri	pã:c
Chattisgarhi	e:k	dui	ti:n	cha:r	pã:ch
Eastern					
Oriya	ek	du'i	tini	chaari	paanjch
Bengali	æk	dui	tin	car	Pãc
Assamese	ek	dui	tini	sari	Pãs
Mayang	a:	du:	tin	sa:ri	pa:z
Elamite					
Elamite+	Ki	--	atbazash		

Northwest					
Brahui	Asi	Ira:	musi	cha:r	Panch
Northeast					
Kurukh	Onta:	emr	mu:nd	na:kh	pance:
Malto	Ort	irw	ti:ne	ca:re	pa:ce
Central					
Kolami	okkod	i:ral	muyal	nallav	Seyyav
Naiki	okko	irotel	muggur	nalgur	
Parji	o:kuri:	irul	mu:ir	nilir	se:vir
Gadaba	okur	iruvul	muvur	naluvur	aydu-gur
Telugu	okati	rendu	muudu	naalugu	Aydu
Gondi	undi:	rend	mu:nd	na:lu:ng	siya:ng
Koya	orro	rendu	mu:n.du	na:lu	a:ydu
Konda	unr̲i	rundi	mu:nr̲i	na:lgi	Aydu
Manda	ru	ri		lalur	Seyyur
Pengo	ro	ri	tin	car	Pãc
Kui	ro	ri	muñji	na:lgi	Singgi
Kuvi	ro:ndi	rindi	ti:ni	sa:ri	pa:sa
South					
Tulu	onji	radd	mu:ji	na:l	Ein
Koraga	onji	raddi	muji	nali	ayni
Kannada	ondu	eraDu	muuru	naaku	aydu
Badaga	ondu	eradu	mu:ru	na:ku	aidu
Kodagu	ond^{ü}	dand^{ü}	mu:nd^{ü}	na:t^{ü}	anji
Kurumba	-onde	-^{e}ddu	-mu.r̲ʉ̲	-na.kʉ̲	-^{e}yidʉ̲
Toda	wïd	e:d	mu:d	no:ng	ýz,
Kota	vodde	yede	mu:nde	na:ke	anje
Tamil	onrru	eranndu	moonrru	naanku	i:ynthu

Malayalam	onnu	rantu	mu:nnu	na:lu	ancu
Irula	vondu	irndu	mura	na:ku	eindu
Nahali					
Nahali	bidum	irar	motho	na:lo	pãco
Burushashki					
Error! Bookmark not defined. Hunza	hik	altó	iskí	wálti	cshindî
Yasin	hek	altó	iskí	wálte	cendî
Basque					
Error! Bookmark not defined. Ancient Basque+	*bade	*biga	*(h)ilur	*laur	*bortz(e)
Basque	bat	bi	hiru	lau	bost
Etruscan					
Etruscan	thu(n)	zal	ci	huth	mach
Hurrian					
Hurrian	--	shin	kig	tumni	---
Meroitic					
Meroitic	--	-tbu	---	---	---

Chart 2 (Numerals from No.6 to No.10)

Languages	**No.6**	**No. 7**	**No.8**	**No.9**	**No.10**
Vedic or Indo European					
Error! Bookmark not defined. Sanskrit	*ṣaṭa*	*sapta*	*aṣṭa/ aṣṭau*	*navam*	*daśam*
Germanic					
Old Germanic+	*seks	*sibum	*ahto:	*niwun	*tehun
Western					

Old English+	sex	seofon	eahta	nighon	Tíen
Middle English+	six	seven	eihte	nien	Ten
English	six	seven	eight	nine	Ten
Scots	sax	seiven	aicht	nyne	Ten
Old Frisian+	sex	sigun	achta	nigun	Tian
W.Frisian	seis	sân	acht	njoggen	Tsien
Frisian (Saterland)	sæks	sogen	oachte	njugen	Tjoon
Dutch	zes	zeven	acht	negen	Tien
W/S Flemish	zèsse	ze:vne	achte	ne:gne	Tiene
Brabants	zes	ze:ve	acht	ne:ge	Ting
Low Saxon	söß	söven	acht	negen	Teihn
Emsland	z*e*s	z*e*:bm	axt	n*e*:ng	Tain
Mennonite Plautdietsch	sass	säwen	acht	näajen	Tian
Afrikaans	ses	sewe	agt	nege	Tien
German	sechs	sieben	acht	neun	Zehn
Central Bavarian	sechse	simme	aochte	naine	Zene
Swabian	sechs	siibe	acht	noen	Zaen
Alsatian	sex	seve	acht	nin	Zehn
Cimbrian	sèks	siban	acht	naün	Zègan
Rimella	zhakshe	shìbne	achtwe	nine	Zìne
Rheinfränkisch	sechs	siwe	acht	nin	Zeen
Pennsylvania	sex	siwwe	acht	nein(e)	Zeh
Luxembourgeois	sechs	siwen	aacht	néng	Zéng
Swiss German	sächs	siebë	acht	nüün	Zäh
Yiddish	zeks	zibn	akht	nayn	Tsen
Middle High German+	sëhs	siben	ahte	niun	Zëhen
Old High	sehs	sibun	ahto	niun	Zehan

German+					
Northern					
Runic+	sæx	siu:	a:tta	ni:u	ti:u
Old Norse+	sex	sjau	átta	níu	tíu
Norwegian	seks	sju	åtte	ni	ti
Danish	seks	syv	otte	ni	ti
Swedish	sex	sju	åtta	nio	tio
Faroese	seks	sjey	átta	níggju	tíggju
Old Icelandic+	sex	siau	átta	nío	tío
Icelandic	sex	sjö	átta	níu	tíu
Eastern					
Gothic+	saíhs	sibun	ahtau	niun	taíhun
Crimean+	seis	sevene	athe	nyne	thiine
Italic					
Oscan+	*sehs	*seften	*uhto	*nuven	*deken
Umbrian+	sehs-			*nuvim	*desem
Faliscan+	zex	*zepte n	octu	*neuen	
Latin+	sex	septem	octo:	novem	decem
Romance					
Mozarabic+	xaix	xebte	oito	(nove)	diex
Portuguese	seis	sete	oito	nove	dez
Galician	seis	sete	oito	nove	dez
Spanish	seis	siete	ocho	nueve	Diez
Ladino	sex	sieti	ochu	muevi	Dies
Asturian	seis	siete	ochu	nueve	Diez
Aragonese	seis	siet	güeito	nueu	Diez
Catalan	sis	set	vuit	nou	Deu
Valencian	sis	set	huit	nou	Deu

Old French+	sis	set	oit	nous	Dis
French	six	sept	huit	neuf	Dix
Walloon	shijh	set	ût	noûf	Dijh
Jèrriais	six	sept	huit	neuf	Dgix
Poitevin	sis	sét	uit	neùv	Dis
Old Picard+	sies	siet	wict	niuf	Deis
Picard	sis	siet	uit	neuf	Dich
Occitan (Provençal)	sièis	sèt	vuèch	nòu	Dètz
Lengadocian	sièis	sèt	uèch	nòu	Dètz
Gascon	shèis	sèt	ueit	nau	Dètz
Auvergnat	siei	sé	veu	neu	Dié
Limosin	siei	se	hue	no:	Die
Franco-Provençal (Vaudois)	sî	sat	houit	nâo	Dyî
Rumantsch Grischun	sis	set	otg	nov	Diesch
Sursilvan	sis	siat	otg	nov	Diesch
Vallader	ses	set	ot	nuov	Desch
Friulian	sîs	syet	vot	nûf	Dîs
Ladin	síes	set	òt	nuéf	Díesc
Dalmatian+	si	sapto	guapto	nu	Dik
Italian	sei	sette	otto	nove	Dieci
Piedmontese	sés	sèt	öt	nöu	Dés
Milanese	sés	sètt	vòtt	noeuv	Dés
Genovese	sei	sette	euttu	neuve	Dexe
Venetian	sié	sete	oto	nove	Diese
Parmesan	s*e*:s	s*e*t	*o*t	n*o*:v	d*e*:z
Corsican	sei	sette	ottu	nove	Dece
Umbrian	séi	sétte	òtto	nòe	Dèsce

Neapolitan	sèië	sèttë	òttë	nòvë	Riécë
Sicilian	sie	setti	òttu	novi	dèci
Romanian	s,ase	s,apte	opt	nouâ	zece
Arumanian	s,ase	s,apte	optu	noauâ	**date**
Meglenite	s,asi	s,apti	uopt	nou	zeti
Istriot	s,åse	s,åpte	opt	devet	deset
Sardinian	ses	sette	otto	nove	deghe
Celtic					
Proto-Celtic+	svex	septn	octô	nevn	decn
Gaulish+	suex	sextan	*oxtû	*navan	decam
Brythonic (P-Celtic)					
Welsh	chwech	saith	wyth	naw	deg
Cardiganshire	sich	soch	nîch	noch	dê
Breton	c'hwec'h	seizh	eizh	nav	dek
Vannetais	huéh	seih	eih	naù	dek
Unified Cornish+	whegh	seyth	eath	naw	dek
Common	hwegh	seyth	eth	naw	deg
Modern	whee	sith	eath	nawe	deeg
Devonian+	hueh	seith	eith	nau	dek
Goidelic (Q-Celtic)					
Old Irish+	se	secht	ocht	noi	Deich
Irish	sé	seacht	ocht	naoi	Deich
Scots Gaelic	sia	seachd	ochd	naoi	Deich
Manx	shey	shiaght	hoght	nuy	Jeih
Hellenic					
Mycenean Greek+	we- (*wex-)			e-ne-wo (*ennewo -)	
Classical Greek+	héx	heptá	októ:	ennéa	Déka

Greek	éksi	eftá	oxtó	ennéa	Dhéka
Cypriot	éksi	eftá	oxtó	eniá	Dhéga
Tsakonian	ékse	eftá	oxtó	enía	Dhéka
Tocharian					
Tocharian A+	**s**äk	**s**pät	okät	ñu	s'äk
Tocharian B+	**s**kas	**s**ukt	okt	ñu	s'ak
Albanian					
Albanian	gjashtë	shtatë	tetë	nëntë	Dhjetë
Gheg (Qosaj)	gh'asht	shtat	tet	nân	Dhet
Tosk (Mandritsa)	g'áshtë	shtátë	tétë	në'ntë	Zjétë
Armenian					
+Classical Armenian	vec^{h}	evt^{h}n	ut^{h}	inn	t'asn
Armenian	vec	yot^{h}	ut^{h}	inn	Tas
Baltic					
West					
Old Prussian+	*usjai	*septi: njai	*asto:nja i	*newi:nj ai	desi:mt an
East					
Lithuanian	sheshì	septynì	ashtuonì	devynì	de:shi mt
Latvian	seshi	septi**n**i	astô**n**i	devi**n**i	Desmit
Latgalian	seshi	septeni	ostoni	deveni	Desmit
Slavic					
East					
Russian	shesth shest'	semh sem'	vósemh vósem'	dévÁth dévyat'	désÁth désyat'
Belarussian	shesthh shesc'	sem sem	vósem vósem	dzévÁth h dzéviac'	dzésÁt hh dzésiac '

Ukrainian	sh--sth shist'	s--m sim	v°s--m vísim	dév'Áth devyat'	désÁth desyat'
West					
Polish	szes'c'	siedem	osiem	dziewie, c'	dziesie, c'
Kashubian	shesc	sétmë	woesmë	dzevjin'c	dzesin' c
Polabian+	sist	sidêm	visêm	diva,t	disa,t
Czech	shest	sedm	osm	devêt	deset
Slovak	shest'	sedem	osem	devät'	desat'
West	shest	sedem	ossem	devat	desat
East	shesc	shedze m	osem	dzevec	dzeshe c
Upper Sorbian	shêsc'	sydom	wosom	dz'ewjec'	dz'esac'
Lower Sorbian	sêsc'	sedym	wosym	z'ewjes'	z'ases'
South					
Old Church Slavonic+	shesti	sedmi	osmi	deve,ti	dese,ti
Bulgarian	shest	sédem	ósem	dévet	Déset
Macedonian	shest	sedum	osum	devet	Deset
Serbo-Croat	shêst	sëdam	ösam	dëve:t	dëse:t
Slovene	shest	sedem	osem	devet	Deset
Anatolian					
Hittite+		shipta-			
Luwian+			*haktau	*nu-	
Lycian+			aitãta	ñuñtãta	
Indo-Iranian					
Proto-Indo-Iranian+	*(k)swac sh	*sapta	*ashta:	*nawa	*daca
Iranian					
Eastern					

Ossetian Iron	æxsæz	avd	ast	farast	Dæs
Digor	æxsæz	avd	ast	farast	Dæs
Avestan+	xshuuash	hapta	ashta	nauua	Dasa
Khwarezmian+	'x	'bhd	'sht	sh'dh	Dhs
Sogdian+	wghwshw	'Bt	'sht	nw'	
Yaghnobi	uxsh	avd	asht	naw	Das
Bactrian+					
Saka+	ksäta'	hauda	ha**st**a	nau	Dasau
Pashto	shpag	ow^{é}	at^{é}	n^{e}	l^{e}s
Wakhi	sha:d	yb	at	na:w	Dhas
Munji	a:xshe	avde	ashkie	nau	Dah
Yidgha	uxsho	avdo	ashcho	nov	Los
Ishkashmi	xu,l	uvd	ot	naw	Da
Sanglechi		haft	ha:**t**		Das
Shughn	xo:gh	wu:vd	waxt	no:w	dhi:s
Rushani	xu:,w	wu:vd	waxt	no:w	Dhes
Yazgulami	xu	uvd	uxt	nu	dhu,s
Sarikoli (Tashkorghani)	xel	üvd	woxt	new	Dhes
Parachi	xi	ho:t	'osht	no:	do:s
Ormuri	sh.^{a}h	ho:	ha:nsht	n^{a}h	Das
Western					
Northwest					
Parthian+	shwh	hft			
Yazdi	shash	haf	hash		
Nayini					De
Natanzi	shæsh	haft	hasht	noh	d'e
Khunsari	shäsh	häft	häsht	no:^{u}	de:^{i}
Gazi	shösh	häf	häsh	nô:^{u}	de:

Sivandi	shush	häf	häsh	nu	da
Vafsi	shish	haf	hash	no	dah
Semnani	shash	haf	hash	na	das
Sangisari	shash	haft	hasht	na	das
Gilaki	shish	haf	hash	noh	da
Mazanderani	shesh	haft	hasht	ne	da
Talysh	shash	håft	hasht	nav	då
Harzani	shosh				doh
Zaza	shesh	**h**ewt	**h**esht	new	des
Gorani	shIsh	hawt	hasht	no	da
Baluchi	sh^{e}sh	h^{e}pt	h^{e}sht	nw	d^{e}h
Turkmenistan	shash	apt	asht	no:	da
E Hill	shash	hapt	hasht	nuh	dah
Rakhshani (Western)	sh^{e}shsh	(h)^{e}pt	(h)^{e}sht	nw	d^e
Kermanji (S) Kurdish	shash	hawt	hasht	no:	da
Zaza (N) Kurdish	shash	haft	hasht	na	Da
Bajalani	shish	ha:ft	hasht	nu:	Da
Kermanshahi	shäsh	häft	häsht	nö^	dé:
Southwest					
Old Persian+			*ashta	*nava	*datha
Pahlavi+	shash	haft	hasht	nuh	Dah
Farsi	shesh	haft	hasht	noh	Dah
Isfahani	shish	haf	hash	no:	Da
Tajik	shash	h=aft	h=asht	nu:h=	dah=
Tati	shæsh	hæft	hæsht	ny"h	Dæh
Chali	shesh	haft	hasht	nö	da:
Fars	shisht	häft	häst	nu	das'a
Lari	Shish	'aft	'asht	no	Da

Luri	Shish	haf	hash	nuh	Dah
Kumzari	Shish	haf'ta	hash'ta	na'hata	da'hata
Nuristani					
Ashkun	**sh**û:	su:t	o:**sht**	**no:**	Dus
Wasi-weri	wu:**sh**	sëtë	a:stë	nu:~	Lezë
Kati	**Sh**u	sut	u**sh**t	nu	Duc
Kalasha-ala	**sh**u:	so:t	o:**sht**	nu:~	do:sh
Indic					
Prakrit+	ch`a	satta	a**tt**a	n.ava	Dasa
Ardhamagadhi+	Cha	satta	a**tt**ha	nava	Dasa
Pali+	Cha	satta	a**tt**ha	nava	Dasa
Romany (Gypsy)					
Spanish	Jol	estér	ostor	nébel	Esden
Welsh	Shov	trin t'a: shto:r	du:vari: shto:r	shto:r t'a: pansh	i desh
Kalderash	Shov	yeftá	oxtó	in'yá	Desh
Syrian	sha:s	h.o:**t**	h.ais**ht**	na:	da:s
Armenian	shesh	haft	ha:sht	nu	Dê
Iranian	Shov	efdá:	óxto	enná	Desh
Sinhalese-Maldivian					
Sinhalese	Haya	hata	ata	namaya	Dahaya
Vedda	pahamay tava ekamay	pahamay dekamay	pahamay tunamay	pahamay hataramay	pahamay tava pahamay
Maldivian	Haie	hate	ashe	nue	Diha
Northern India					
Dardic					
Kashmiri	shah	sat	$^{e:}$**th**	naw	da
Shina	**sh**a	sât	Â~**sh**	nau~	daï

Brokskat	**s**a	sa:t̲	A:**st**	nu	da:sh
Phalura	**sho**^{h}	sa:t	A:**sht**	nu:~	da:sh
Bashkarik	sho:	sat	a**t**h	num	dash
Tirahi	xo	sat	axt	nab	dah
Torwali	sho:	sat	a**t**	no:m	dash
Wotapuri	sho:	sat	a**t**	nau	dash
Maiya	sho:h	sa:t	a:**t**h	nau~	dash
Kalasha	**sho**	sat	a**sht**	nõ	dash
Khowar	chhoy	sot	osht	nyuf	josh
Dameli	**sho**	sat	a**sh**t	nõ:	dash
Gawar-bati	**sh**^{u}o:	s^{e}t	o:**st**	nu:~	dosh
Pashai	**ch**ha	sa:ta	a:**sht**a	na:w	da:y
Shumashti	**shoo**	sa	â**sht**	nu:	däs
Nangalami	**s**o:	sat	õ:**st**	nu:~	das
Dumaki	**sh**a	sot	o**sh**t	nau	dai
Western					
Marathi	s^{e}ha	sat	a**t**h	n^{e}u	d^{e}ha
Konkani	sô	sat	atth	nov	dha
Sindhi	cha	sata	atha	nava	**dd**aha
Khatri	cho	sat	a**t**h	nu	Dô
Lahnda	ch\`e:	satt	**att**\`	nå~	**d**a:h
Central					
Hindi/ Urdu	c^{h}ai	sa:t	a:**t**h	nau	Das
Parya	ch^{h}e	sat	a**t**	nu	Das
Punjabi	che	s^{e}t	^{e}**t**	n^{e}wng	d^{e}s
Siraiki	chi	sat	a**t**h	naõ	Dah
Gujarati	ch^{e}	sat	a**t**h	n^{e}v	d^{e}s
Rajasthani (Marwari)	ch\`aw	sa:t	a:**t**\`	naw	Das

Banjari (Lamani)	Cho	saat	aaT	naw	Das
Malvi	ch`e:	sa:t	a:**t**`	naw	Das
Bhili	so:	xa:t	a:**t**`	naw	Dax
Dogri	ch`e:	sat	a**t**`	nau	Das
Kumauni	ch`ai	sa:t	a:**t**`	nau	Das
Garhwali	ch`ai:	sa:t	a:**t**`	nau	Das
W Pahari	tsho:	sa:**t**	a:**t**:h	no:	do:sh
Khandeshi	ch`a	sa:t	a:**t**`	naü	Das
East Central					
Nepali	Cha	sa:t	a:**t**	nau	Das
Maithili	ch`a:	sa:t	a:**t**'	náu	Dash
Magahi	Chau	sat	a:th	nau	Das
Bhojpuri	c^{h}æ	sa:t	a:**t**^{h}	nao	Das
Awadhi (Kosali)	cha:	sa:t	a:th	nuu	Dus
Chattisgarhi	ch`e:	sa:t	a:**t**`	no:	Das
Eastern					
Oriya	cha'a	saat	aa**t**h	na'a	Dash
Bengali	choy	sat	a**t**	noy	Dosh
Assamese	s^{e}i	xat	ath	n^{e}	d^{e}h
Mayang	soy	ha:d	a:t	nau	Dos
Elamite					
Elamite+					
Northwest					
Brahui	shash	haft	hasht	no:	Dah
Northeast					
Kurukh	soyye:	satte:	a**tt**he:	nai**m**ye:	dasse:
Malto	so:ye	sa:te	a:**te**	noye	da:se
Central					

Kolami	saa / a:r	sa.t	a.t	nov	daa
Naiki					
Parji	se:je:n				
Gadaba	a:ru-gur				padi-mandi
Telugu	aaru	eedu	enimidi	tommidi	padi
Gondi	sa:ru:ng	e:**ru**:ng	armur	anma	putth
Koya	a:ru	e:**d**u	ennimidi	tommidi	padi
Konda	a:ru	e:**ru**			
Manda					
Pengo	co	sa**t**	at	nov	das
Kui	sajgi	odgi	a:**t**u	na	dashu
Kuvi	so:	sa:ta	a:**ta**	no:	dos
South					
Tulu	a:ji	**e:**l	e**n**ma	ormba	patt
Koraga	aji	eli			pattu
Kannada	aaru	eeLu	eNTu	ombattu	Hattu
Badaga	a:ru	iyyu	e**tt**u	ombattu	Attu
Kodagu	a:r$^{\ddot{u}}$	ye:**l**$^{\ddot{u}}$	ye**tt**$^{\ddot{u}}$	oyimbad ü	patt$^{\ddot{u}}$
Kurumba	-a.rʉ̲	-ö.**l**ʉ̲	-ö**tt**ʉ̲	-embadʉ̲	-pattʉ̲
Toda	o:**r**	öw	öt	Wïnboth	Pot
Kota	a:re	ye:ye	ye**tt**e	vorapa:de	Patte
Tamil	aarru	aezhu	a:ddu	Onpathu	paththu
Malayalam	a:**r**u	e:**l**u	e**tt**u	Onpatu	Pattu
Irula	aru	elu	yettu	vombadu	Pattu
Nahali					
Nahali	cha:h	sato	a**th**o	Nav	Das
Burushashki					
Error!	mishíndi	thalé	altámbi	Huntí	Tóorimi

Bookmark not defined. Hunza					
Yasin	bishínde	thalé	altámbe	Hutí	Tórom
Basque					
Error! Bookmark not defined. Ancient Basque+				bade-eratsi	
Basque	sei	Zazpi	zortzi	bederatzi	Hamar
Etruscan					
Etruscan	sa	semph	Cezp	enva?	Zar
Hurrian					
Hurrian	--	shindia	--	Nizhi	Eman
Meroitic					
Meroitic					

Initial Mutations

(A Characteristic Feature of Vedic Family of Languages)

1. Vedic language

Since Vedic Sanskrit was a spoken language, its phonetics was not stable. Ablauts (vowel interchanges), assimilations, many different consonant processes at the end of the word were the main features developed in various branch languages developed from Vedic Sanskrit from time to time. We may find out the trend of development of Vedic phonetics in its branches. These things can only be seen in comparison of different branches and groups with their own phonetic peculiarities. Here we shall try to highlight the trend of initial mutations in the leading Vedic family of languages.

Gradation of vowel in initial position is found in the Vedic language structure. The most common example of this is the case of *a* - in some words. It sometimes disappears but sometimes remains as it was, and linguists know that the word for "a bone" sounded in the Vedic language is *Asthi. Asthi* becomes *kost-* in Balto-Slavic, *ost-* in Celto-Italic. It is *hast-* in Hittite, *odb* in Old Irish, *os, ossis* in Latin, though it had also *costa* (a rib), *kost* in Russian etc. It seems probable that different dialects of the Vedic language might be having different variant of the same stem.

The initial *k-*, as well as other fricative sounds, is also seen disappearing in some other words. The same process was common for the initial *s-*. It can disappear rarely, but still, we think, regularly. There are two versions of this phenomenon's origin. Some believe it occurred due to the prefix *s-* with unclear meaning; some state this is a "*sandhi*", the influence of the previous word ending in *-s*. The last sound causes a change of the initial one in the next word, and that is called "*sandhi*" from Sanskrit, where it is very common.

But the above mentioned cases are the only ones in Vedic languages, where we can speak for sure about the initial mutations.

2. Anatolian languages

Hittite, Luwian and Palaic languages are interesting for they drifted apart from the Vedic language community shortly before the Vedic language took its latest forms. Anatolian languages bear features that are too similar to Vedic language. Initial mutations can be located in them. Hittite shows *k* changing into - *h* that is the peculiarity of Sanskrit language. We should bear in mind that Anatolian languages suffered really great changes while contacting with Hatti, Aramaeans and other aboriginal nations of Asia. The dictionary of Hittite has got only about 22% of purely Vedic language family words, other ones are of Hatti and other origins. The religious system and terms is almost completely borrowed from aborigines. Many changes took place in phonetics as well. That is, we believe, the case with *k* >*h* mutation in initial position. Sanskrit *Kara* (hand) was pronounced in Hittite as *keššar* (a hand) and also as *hiššari*. That initial *h* disappeared completely in Luwian.

The other mutation is even more interesting, for it has strange and mysterious analogues in Baltic, Slavic and Italic languages. We speak about the change *n* > *l* >*t* and we offer you a word *lamen* (to name) derived from Vedic language *nāma-* (a name). A derivative from that Hittite verb was *a-timan* (a name), which makes us think about the instability of the initial sound in that verb in Anatolian languages. It seems that in some cases - exactly still unknown - Vedic *n-* was so unstable and weak that easily could turn into *l-* (obviously, a palatal sound) and *t-* (palatal, too). Another example, this time from Luwian, will be *tapaša* (sky) which sounded *nepiš* in Hittite and *nabha-* in Vedic language. The same law *n* >*t* acts here.

And the third mutation that was also irregular in the language: *d* >*t* >*š* which we will analyze in Hittite and Luwian with only one example. The Vedic *devas* (star or daylight) was used to denote stars in the Vedas. *Devas* was worshipped among Anatolians as well, and was called *tiwat* (sun god) in Luwian, and *tijaz, tiuna* (a god) in Palaic. That happens according to common Anatolian phonetic laws. But in Hittite, nevertheless, this god's name was like *šiu, šiun*, and the word for "a day" cognate to it was *šiwat*. In Sanskrit 'a day' is called as '*divas*'. We don't know for sure if this initial consonant really sounded as English [sh], that is why the hypothesis exists that that was a sibilant close to palatal [d], seen in Ancient Umbrian.

§ 3. Slavic and Baltic languages.

The *n>d* problem exists in both Baltic and Slavic branches, long ago being united in Balto-Slavic community. We shall note that neither Baltic, nor Slavic languages have now or had ever had initial mutations depending on the previous words or sounds. No regular signs of it are noticed, and nevertheless some examples exist, being quite irregular and too scarce in those languages.

The Lithuanian *namas* (a house) is obviously derived from Vedic *damas-* (a house), also seen in Russian *dom*, Latin *domus*, Greek domos, Germanic *tum-*. This Lithuanian word has a *n-* which points out the nature of mutation being vice-verse.

The next example is the same as in Luwian mentioned above. The Vedic word for "sky", *nabha-*, turned in Lithuanian into *debesis* (a cloud), though it is *nebo, nebesa* in Russian etc. As we can see here, the mutation is vise versa: *n >d.* It is evident that these initial *n* and *d* were too weak to keep their place and had to change or interchange, replaced by each other, both being dental sounds in parent Vedic language.

And the third case we would like to point here is concerned both Slavic and Baltic languages: the word *devyni* (nine) in Lithuanian originated from Vedic *navan.* The only explanation of this particular phenomenon is the influence of the next numeral "ten" which sounds in Vedic as *daśa* and *daśam* or in Slavic *desert.* But still, if this really happened, it proves the weakness of the initial *n-* in this word, so it was easily converted into *d-*.

Now let's remember Hittite *n > l* mutation, because the similar one can be met in Baltic tongues. Vedic language *nīḍa-* (a nest) in all branches has a *n-* in the beginning of it. All but Baltic which show *lizdas* ("a nest" in Lithuanian). Again the similarity which makes us think there was something in Vedic language that in certain cases mutated the initial consonants.

§ 4. Italic languages.

So we see that every irregular phonetic mutation mentioned above is rotating around *d, n, t, l* sounds. This is natural, because exactly these four sounds are dentals and that's why have much in common in articulation while being pronounced. We summed up cases met in Hittite, Luwian, Palaic, Lithuanian, Common Slavic. Now is the turn of Latin.

In fact, we have two examples to fit the matter being discussed. The first one is concerned the word *lacrima* (a tear) that obviously comes from Italic *dacerma* which comes from Vedic *Dṛṇāti*. So *d* > *l*, and this feature cannot at all be called regular, as all other known words in *l-* with Vedic origin have their ancestor stem beginning with the same letter. Let's remember *lacus* (a lake), *liber* (free, free people), *lupus* (a wolf), *longus* (long). They all have cognates in other Vedic languages with this very ***l-*** at the beginning.

§ 5. Celtic Languages

And now we may see initial consonant mutations. Insular Celtic languages. These mutations became one of their characteristic features. Let us have some typical examples from all those Insular Celtic tongues.

1. *doras* - a door from Vedic *dvāra*
   mo dhoras - my door (pronounced [goras], with a sort of Greek "gamma")
   bhur ndoras - your door (pronounced [noras])

2. *benen* - a woman from Vedic *Vāmā*
   an venen - the woman

It seems that Vedic language never entertained initial mutations. But its branches developed this feature owing to different geographical backgrounds.

Review of the idea of Classification of IE Languages as Centum and Satam group

Thus we have seen in the foregoing pages the entire laws right from the evolution of phonemes through monosyllabic roots till the origin of Vedic language were discovered and defined by the Vedic seers. But the European scholars discarded all these laws in their religious and political interests and wasted their precious time in giving birth to a Language which never existed in the world and to study the existing languages in the light of the usage of the speculated Proto Indo-European Language (PIL).

We may give here an example of the wastage of precious time by the scholars who studied the Vedic group of languages in the name of Indo-European languages (IE) in the light of a speculated PIL instead of the extant Vedic Language. In c.1870 Prof. Ascoly carried out a study on the numerals of 100 recorded into various Vedic (so called IE) languages. The following is the position of numerals denoting 100 in various Vedic (IE) languages.

Sanskrit	:	*śatam*
Avesta	:	satam
Persian	:	sada
Hindi	:	sau
Russian	:	sto
Lithuanian	:	szimtas
Latin	:	Centum
Greek	:	Hekaton
Irish	:	Cet
Tocharian	:	Kandh
Gothic	:	Hund
German:	Hundret	

French	:	Cent
Italian	:	Kento
English	:	Hundred, Cent and

In PIL the numeral for 100 was speculated as 'kmtom'

In view of the above position of the numerals denoting 100 in various Vedic (IE) languages and speculated "kmtom" in the so called PIL language, Prof. Ascoly found two types of trends.

1). That either PIE guttro-palatal sounds (kya, khy, gy, ghy) convert into guttural sounds (k, kh, g, gh) into some of the IE languages or

2). They convert into sibilant sounds (s, z) into other IE languages.

On the basis of thsese two types of trends of conversion, he classified the IE languages into two groups : Centum and Satam. Centum group of languages contains languages like Latin, Greek, Irish, Tocharian, Gothic, German, French, Italian etc. But the readers will find that Ascoly was not able to define the origin of aspiration (h) in the Gothic "hund", German "hundred" and Greek "hekaton" from PIE guttro-palatal "kmtom". According to the rules of classification by Ascoly, Greek, German and Gothic cannot be classified into Centum group of Languages. For the languages like Greek, Gothic and German, there should have been some other group defined and probably named as hentum or hektum. The most surprising thing is that English records both cent and hundred for 100. Thus English represents both satam and hektum.

The most unfortunate thing is that since 1870, this unfounded idea is being taught and studied by scholars into the universities in the name of linguistics without going into the depth of the things placed forward by Ascoly.

Whereas the above trend of languages can better be defined in the light of Vedic (Sanskrit) language. It can be observed that Sanskrit palatal sibilant (śatam) was retained as dental sibilant in some of its branches like Avesta, Persian, Russian, Lithuanian, French etc. and it changed into guttural sounds in the languages like Latin, Irish, Tocharian and Italian. If we go by Pāṇinian rule

8.2.62, we shall find that Sanskrit ś changes into 'k' in Sanskrit itself. e.g. *diś* becomes *dik*. It tells guttralisation of palatal sibiant. Under the same rule we can study the conversion of Sanskrit sibilant into guttral sound into the Latin, Irish, Tocharian and Italian languages. Similarly according to Pāṇini -7.4.52, 's' changes to 'h' into the example of '*edhitāhe*'. This tendency can be registered into various other Vedic (IE) languages where 's' has transposed into 'h'. This way the tendency of German, Gothic, Greek and English languages of converting Sanskrit 's' into 'h' can be studied into the above cited Pāṇinian rule.

Thus foregoing discussion exposes the Early European scholarship. The great work had already taken place in India to deal with the linguistic tendencies, but the European scholars due to their vested religious interests and superiority complex set aside all these genuine studies done in India and tried to set their own rules to establish the authenticity of speculated language. Now one can easily know how shallow is the idea of classifying the languages into centum and satam groups. All these languages are the offshoots of Sanskrit and the phonological changes have taken in these languages also following the rules already discussed in detail by Pāṇini and other phoneticians of ancient India.

In view of the 'Vedic Theory of the origin of language' it can be stated that languages retaining 's' sounds and converting 's' into 'h' (Greek, Gothic, German etc) originated first from Sanskrit, where as languages converting 's' into 'k' (Latin, Tocharian, Italian etc) originated later from Sanskrit.

In addition to the above review, it is necessary to review all such Laws based upon the speculated PIL

Review of Grimm's Law

Grimm's Law is one of the most important laws that can be discussed here. This law is also known in German as Lautverschiebung or the law of sound-shifting. Prof. Max Müller called it as Grimm' Law as the same was described in detail by Jacob Grimm in 1822 in his German Grammar titled as "Deustche Grammatik". But Otto Jespersen in his book Language (P.43) emphasised that this law should be known as Rask's law by the name of a Danish scholar Rask who first pointed it out in his book *Undersogelse.* His observations are given as under: "If any one is to give his name to this law, a better name would be 'Rask's Law'. Thus the nomenclature of this law has always been a bone of contention.

Grimm's Law can be divided into two parts. First part deals with the first sound shifting and second part deals with the second sound shifting. According to the law of first sound shifting, PIL sounds of 'gh', 'dh', 'bh', 'g', 'd', 'b', 'k', 't', 'p' are retained in Sanskrit, Greek, Latin and Slav languages as it is, but they are shifted in Germanic languages (Gothic, Low German, English and Dutch) in 'g', 'd', 'b', 'k', 't', 'p', 'kh', 'th', 'ph' respectively. Here it may be noted that the examples given to illustrate this shifting are generally quoted from Sanskrit instead of speculated PIL. For instance, Sanskrit '*bhrātṛ*' becomes 'brude' in German, 'brother' in English and 'brawd in Velsh. Here in all these examples Skt. 'bh' changes into 'b'. Similarly Skt. '*vidhavā*' becomes in English as 'widow owing to the change of 'dh' into 'd'. Skt. '*hansa* (*ghansa*) becomes in English as 'goose'. Here it may be pointed out that this tendency does not hold true in case of so called hypothetical PIL, but it holds true in case of Sanskrit only which is available today in its extant form. Moreover, the above law was not some new law discovered by so called Grimms or Rasks, but defined thousands of years of ago by Pāṇini himself. According to Pāṇini (*jhalāṁ jaśo'nte*-8.2.39 and *jhalāṁ jasa jhasi*-8.4.52), voiced aspirate sounds like 'jh', 'bh', 'gh', 'ḍh', 'dh' are deaspirated,i.e. converted into j, b, g, ḍ, and d respectively. Similarly Pāṇini's rule (*khari ca*-8.4.55) mentions the devoicing process of voiced sounds. That is change of 'g', 'd', 'b', 'j', 'ḍ' into 'k', 't', 'p', 'c', and 'ṭ' respectively. Under this rule vāg>vā'k, tad>tat, ab> ap. Similarly owing to the same rule Skt. go>English 'cow'; Skt. yug> English yoke; Skt. daśa> English ten; Skt. dvau>Eng. two; Skt. ad > Eng. eat etc. Third round of this sound shift has also been recorded by Vārttikakāra (*cayo dvitīyāḥ śari pauṣkarasādeḥ* on Paṇini-8.4.48). Accordingly, voiceless unaspirates change into voiceless aspirates, i.e. 'k', 'ṭ', 't', 'p' change respectively into 'kh', 'ṭh', 'th', 'ph'. Skt. example is *vatsara*. Owing to this rule of aspiration of voiceless unaspirate sounds following sound shifting from Skt. to other IE languages may be defined. For instance, Skt. *tri*> Eng. Three; Skt. *trayas*> Gothic threis, thrija; Skt. *pitṛ*>German vater, Eng. father; Skt. *mātṛ*>Old Irish māthir; Skt. *tṛṇa*> Eng. Thorn; Skt. *tanu*> Eng.

thin; Skt. pāda>Eng. foot. Thus from the foregoing it is crystal clear that this rule has already been discussed by Pāṇini hundreds of years ago when Grimms and Rasks were not even born. As such firstly this is the Sanskrit phonetician's rule of deaspiration, devoicing and aspiration of voiceless aspirate sounds. Secondly, this rule has nothing to do with PIL, but applies accurately with Sanskrit as the mother language of the entire European Vedic family of languages.

Vedic Family of Languages

- Indian
    - Sanskrit Pali and Prakrits > Apbhranshas > Other Indian languages like Bengali and Hindi
- Iranian
    - **Avestan**
    - Old Persian -> Modern Persian
- Armenian
- Balto-Slavic
    - Baltic -> Prussian, Lettish, Lithuanian
    - Slavic
        - West -> Polish, Czecho-Slovak
        - South -> Bulgarian, Slovenian, Serbo-Croatian
        - East -> Russian
- Albanian
- Celtic -> Gallic
    - Gaelic -> Old Irish (-> Scots Gaelic, Irish Gaelic, Manx)
    - Brittanic -> Old Welsh (-> Welsh, Cornish, Breton, Pictish)
- Germanic
    - North (Old Norse) -> Norwegian, Icelandic, Danish, Swedish
    - East -> Gothic
    - West
        - Anglo-Frisian
            - Old Frisian
            - Old English

                - Mercian -gt; Midland Dialect -> East Midland Dialect -> Early Modern English -> Modern English
                - Northumbrian -> Northern Dialect -> Lowland Scots
                - Kentish
                - West Saxon -> Southern Dialect -> Dorsetshire Dialect
        - German
            - Low -> Old Saxon -> Plattdeutsch, Old Low Franconian (-> Dutch, Flemish)
            - High -> Modern Standard German

- Italic
    - Oscan
    - Umbrian
    - Latin
        - Portuguese
        - Spanish
        - Old French -> Norman French, Modern French
        - Italian
        - Roumanian
- Hellenic
    - Doric
    - Aeolic
    - Ionic-Attic -> Greek (Koine)
- Hittite
- Tocharian

References

1. *Āpastamba Śrauta Sūtra* (*Āśs.*), 1953 : ed. Vidwan T. Shriniwas Gopalacharya, Mysore.

2. (i) (Dr.) Arya, Ravi Prakash, 2007 : *Vedic and Classical Sanskrit.* Indian Foundation for Vedic Science, Delhi.

(ii) (Dr.) Arya, Ravi Prakash, 1991 : *Researches into Vedic and Linguistic Studies*, Grantha Bharati Prakashan, Delhi.

3. (Dr.) Bhārtiya, Bhawanilal Vs. 2042: *Pūnā Pravacana,* Vedic Pustakalaya, Ajmer.

4. (Dr.) Gopal, Ram 1983 : *History and Principles of Vedic interpretations.* Concept Publishing company. Delhi.

5. (It. Col.) Kennedy. Vans 1828 : *Researches into the Origin and Affinity of the Principal languages of Asia and Europe.* London.

6. Monier Williams, M : *A Sanskrit English Dictionary*, Motilal Banarssidas, Delhi, 2002.

7. Macdonell, A. A. : *A Vedic Grammar*, Strassburg, 1910.

8. *Nirukta* (*Nir.*) : Nirukta of Yāska, Ed. Rajawade, V.K. Poona, BORI, 1940.

9. Pāṇini (Pāṇ.): *Aṣṭādhyāyī.* Chowkhamba Sanskrit series office, Varanasi. 1950.

10. *Ṛgveda* (*RV.*): Ed. & Tr. in Sanskrit and Hindi by Swami Dayanand, Ajmer.

11. *Satyārtha Prakash* (S.P.): By Swami Dayanand. Saraswati. Ramlal Kapoor Trust, Bahalgarh, Haryana, 1974.

12. Serjeantson, Mary S. 1935: *A History of Foreign words*

in English, London.

13. *Vārttika (Vār.):* Kāryāyana's *vārttikas* on Pāṇinian *Sūtras*. See Mabābhāṣya ed. Vedavrata, Rohtak, Haryana. 1963.

14. Wackerganel, J. : *Altindische Grammatik*, Göttingen, Vandenhock & Ruprecht, 1954.

15. Whitney W.D.: *Sanskrit Grammar*, Harward, 1955.

www.ingramcontent.com/pod-product-compliance
Lightning Source LLC
Chambersburg PA
CBHW060826050426
42453CB00008B/602
* 9 7 8 8 1 8 7 7 1 0 6 1 5 *